D1299077

COUNTRIES OF THE WORLD

Tanzania

Gareth Stevens Publishing
A WORLD ALMANAC EDUCATION GROUP COMPANY

About the Author: Wairagala Wakabi is a staff writer with *The EastAfrican*, a regional online weekly newspaper published in Kenya. He also writes for a number of international publications. Wakabi holds a master of arts degree in journalism and media studies from Rhodes University of South Africa.

Written by
WAIRAGALA WAKABI

Edited by
PATRICIA NG

Edited in the U.S. by
CATHERINE GARDNER
ALAN WACHTEL

Designed by
GEOSLYN LIM

Picture research by
THOMAS KHOO
JOSHUA ANG

First published in North America in 2005 by
Gareth Stevens Publishing
A World Almanac Education Group Company
330 West Olive Street, Suite 100
Milwaukee, Wisconsin 53212 USA

Please visit our web site at
www.garethstevens.com
For a free color catalog describing
Gareth Stevens Publishing's list of high-quality
books and multimedia programs, call
1-800-542-2595 (USA) or 1-800-387-3178 (Canada)
Gareth Stevens Publishing's fax: (414) 332-3567.

© **MARSHALL CAVENDISH INTERNATIONAL (ASIA)**
PRIVATE LIMITED 2004
Originated and designed by
Times Editions Marshall Cavendish
An imprint of Marshall Cavendish International (Asia) Pte Ltd
A member of Times Publishing Limited
Times Centre, 1 New Industrial Road
Singapore 536196
http://www.timesone.com.sg/te

Library of Congress Cataloging-in-Publication Data
Wakabi, Wairagala.
Tanzania / by Wairagala Wakabi.
p. cm. — (Countries of the world)
Includes bibliographic references and index.
ISBN 0-8368-3119-5 (lib. bdg.)
1. Tanzania—Juvenile literature.
I. Title. II. Countries of the world (Milwaukee, Wis.)
DT438.W35   2004
967.8—dc22   2004045265

Printed in Singapore

1 2 3 4 5 6 7 8 9 08 07 06 05 04

PICTURE CREDITS

Agence France Presse: 15, 16, 17, 36, 37, 75, 82, 83, 85
Art Directors & TRIP Photo Library: 3 (bottom), 9 (top), 28, 52, 58, 59, 61
Corbis: 38, 51, 54, 62, 67, 73, 76, 80
David Cumming/Eye Ubiquitous: 3 (top), 12, 68, 69, 91
U. Doering/AfriPics: 78
Focus Team—Italy: 3 (center), 4, 19, 27, 33, 34, 43, 57
David Forman/Eye Ubiquitous: 8
HBL Network: 2, 12 (top), 18, 22, 26, 32, 35, 48, 89
Dave G. Houser/Houserstock: 56
The Hutchison Library: 6, 14, 15 (top), 23, 25, 40, 42, 47, 63
Laure Communications: 10, 11, 20, 65
Lonely Planet Images: 29, 77
James Mollison/Eye Ubiquitous: 36 (top)
Bob Pateman: 1, 7, 21, 41, 53
Mike Powles/Eye Ubiquitous: 9, 87
Tanzanite Foundation: 44, 45
Travel Ink: 7, 13, 19 (top)
Audrius Tomonis – www.banknotes.com: 90 (both)
Topham Picturepoint: 30, 39, 55, 64, 84
U.S. Peace Corps 81
A. van Zandbergen/AfriPics: 31, 79
Nik Wheeler: 5, 24, 30 (top), 46, 49, 50, 60, 66, 71, 74
William Wheeler/Houserstock: 59 (top)
Alison Wright: cover, 70, 72

Digital Scanning by Superskill Graphics Pte Ltd

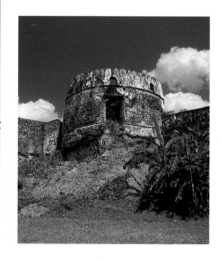

Contents

AN OVERVIEW OF TANZANIA

The United Republic of Tanzania was formed when the Republic of Tanganyika merged with the Republic of Zanzibar in 1964. Julius Nyerere, the country's first president, implemented many policies aimed at increasing economic growth and promoting self-sufficiency. Today, however, Tanzania is still one of the poorest nations in the world.

Tanzania's most famous landmark is Mount Kilimanjaro, the highest point on the entire African continent. The country is also home to the Olduvai Gorge, where fossils of ancient humans have been discovered. The beautiful island of Zanzibar is world renowned as an exotic tourist destination because of its sandy beaches and rich cultural history.

Opposite: **Crested cranes make their home at the Arusha National Park, alongside a wide variety of birds and wildlife.**

Below: **Sultan Seyyid Barghash built the Marahubi Palace in Zanzibar as a home for his harem. It was accidently burned down in 1899. Today, all that stands are its ruins.**

THE FLAG OF TANZANIA

The national flag of Tanzania combines elements from both the flag of Tanganyika and the flag of Zanzibar. The bottom green band of the Tanganyika flag was replaced with the top blue band of the Zanzibari flag. All the stripes were then rearranged in a diagonal manner to give each one equal status. The green portion in the upper left-hand corner of the flag represents the land, while the blue portion in the bottom right-hand corner represents the adjoining sea. The diagonal black stripe running through the flag stands for the people, while the yellow bands on either side of the black stripe stand for the mineral wealth of the country.

Geography

Located in East Africa, Tanzania is bordered to the north by Kenya and Uganda, to the northwest by Burundi and Rwanda, to the west by the Democratic Republic of the Congo (DRC), to the southwest by Zambia, to the south by Mozambique and Malawi, and to the east by the Indian Ocean. The country, which includes the islands of Mafia, Pemba, and Zanzibar, has an area of 364,900 square miles (945,087 square kilometers) and has a coastline of 885 miles (1,424 km).

Opposite: **The Great Ruaha River eventually joins the Rufiji River and flows toward the Indian Ocean.**

Mountains and Valleys

The East African Rift System extends into Tanzania in two branches. One branch is the Western Rift Valley, which runs along the western border of Tanzania and includes Lakes Tanganyika and Rukwa. The other branch, the Eastern Rift Valley, runs through central Tanzania, beginning at the Kenyan border in the region of Lakes Natron, Eyasi, and Manyara, and moving southward to Lake Nyasa and the border with Mozambique. Between these two branches is the Central Plateau, which covers one third of Tanzania.

Below: **The Ngorongoro Conservation Area was added to the World Heritage List in 1979 by the United Nations Educational, Scientific, and Cultural Organization (UNESCO). This area boasts a large variety of wildlife.**

The Ufipa Plateau, the Mbeya Range, and Mount Rungwe form a highland range in the southwest. Along the country's coast are the Usambara and Pare Mountain Ranges. Tanzania is home to Mount Kilimanjaro, which rises to a height of 19,340 feet (5,895 meters), making it the highest mountain on the African continent. To the northwest of Kilimanjaro is Mount Meru, which is 14,980 feet (4,566 m) high.

Rivers and Lakes

Tanzania shares Lake Victoria, the world's second-largest freshwater lake, with Kenya and Uganda. Lake Tanganyika, the second-deepest lake in the world, forms part of Tanzania's border with Burundi and the DRC, while Lake Nyasa forms part of Tanzania's border with Malawi. Other major lakes in the country include Lakes Eyasi, Manyara, and Natron, in the northeast, and Lake Rukwa, in the southwest.

The major rivers in Tanzania include the Pangani, the Rufiji, the Ruvuma, and the Wami. All four flow into the Indian Ocean. Another major river, the Kagera, drains into Lake Victoria. All the country's minor rivers flow into basins created by the rift valley.

KILIMANJARO: THE ROOF OF AFRICA

Mount Kilimanjaro is the tallest mountain in Africa. Kibo (*below*) is the tallest of Kilimanjaro's three peaks. It has a permanent snowcap.
(A Closer Look, page 58)

Climate

The climate in Tanzania is mainly tropical, with the hot season lasting from November to February and the cold season from May to August. The elevation of the land, however, tends to create variations in temperature. Highland temperatures reach only as high as 68° Fahrenheit (20° Celsius) in the hot season and as low as 50° F (10° C) in the cold season. The temperatures in the rest of the country range between 77° F and 86° F (25° C and 30° C) in the hot season and 59° F and 68° F (15° C and 20° C) in the cold season.

Tanzania's coastal areas receive the most rainfall in the country, mainly during two periods — October to December and March to May. About half of Tanzania receives less than 30 inches (75 centimeters) of rain each year. The yearly rainfall in many highland areas is greater than 60 inches (152 cm). The Central Plateau is the country's driest area, receiving an average of less than 20 inches (51 cm) of rainfall annually. The plateau's rainy season is between December and May.

Temperatures on Pemba and Zanzibar Islands are similar to those on the mainland. The rainfall, however, is greater. The annual rainfall figures for Zanzibar and Pemba are 60 inches (152 cm) and 80 inches (203 cm), respectively.

Below: **During the dry season, the water level of the Great Ruaha River runs low.**

Left: Gazelles roam freely in the various national parks of Tanzania.

ENDANGERED ELEPHANTS

Elephant tusks are a source of ivory, a valuable material used to make statues and other decorative objects. Although most African nations, including Tanzania, do not officially trade in ivory or ivory products, wildlife authorities are certain that a small number of poachers continue to operate in Africa.

(A Closer Look, page 50)

Plants and Animals

Tanzania's diverse landscape and climate contribute to the wide range of plant life in the country. Forests can be found in the highland areas, where rainfall is more abundant. In areas with less rainfall, bushes and thickets grow. Grassland tends to grow in areas that have been used for growing crops or grazing animals or areas that have few rivers. Swamps form in areas that flood perennially, and deserts can be found at high altitudes and in areas with little rain.

The open spaces and low population densities in Tanzania have allowed a variety of wildlife to flourish. Animals, ranging from predators such as hyenas, leopards, and lions, to hoofed animals, such as buffalo, gazelles, giraffes, gnu, and zebras, roam Tanzania's many national parks, conservation areas, game reserves, and game-controlled areas. Civet cats and mongooses can be found on the islands of Pemba and Zanzibar.

The river banks and lake shores support crocodiles and hippopotamuses. Conservation efforts protect rhinoceroses and elephants from poachers.

THE WONDERS OF THE SERENGETI

The Serengeti region is home to remarkable plant and animal life, such as the waterbuck (*below*). Most of the Serengeti region is in Tanzania, but it also extends into Kenya.

(A Closer Look, page 70)

History

Tanganyika's Early Days

Fossil remains found in the Olduvai Gorge show that prehistoric life existed in the northern part of the region that became Tanganyika and, later, Tanzania. It is known that indigenous groups existed in the interior, but little is known about them. Arabs were the earliest known visitors to the coast of the region and were interested primarily in trade. In search of slaves to trade, the Arabs explored the interior and discovered ivory. They progressed inward until they came into conflict with Mirambo, an African chief who cut off the Arabs' trade routes when they refused to pay him a tribute.

The Portuguese arrived in the late fifteenth century and gained power over the Arabs by taking control of the entire coast. The Portuguese were driven out of this area in the eighteenth century, with help from the Arabs, by the indigenous groups along the coast.

The British began their explorations of Tanganyika in the 1840s. The Germans arrived in the 1880s. The 1886 Anglo-German Agreement divided the interior of East Africa between the British

BAGAMOYO'S SLAVE TRADE

The town of Bagamoyo has a long, historic, and infamous past. Once a thriving center for the slave trade and government, Bagamoyo has since faded into a quiet coastal town.
(A Closer Look, page 48)

Below: Erected in 1700, the Old Fort was built to defend the Arabs from Portuguese attacks. Later, it became a prison and, then, a railroad depot. Now, it is a cultural center.

Left: **Julius Nyerere during his first speech as prime minister of the Republic of Tanganyika.**

EXPLORING THE OLDUVAI GORGE

Olduvai Gorge is one of the world's most famous archaeological sites. It is part of an area added to the UNESCO World Heritage List in 1979.
(*A Closer Look, page 52*)

and the Germans. While they were in charge of the area that became Tanganyika, the Germans helped to develop coffee and rubber industries, schools, and a railroad. Colonial rule, however, did not agree with the indigenous or the Arab groups, and many uprisings, such as the Maji Maji Rebellion of 1905, occurred.

In 1919, after World War I, the Treaty of Versailles awarded Britain a League of Nations mandate to take Tanganyika from the Germans. The British retained control of the area until a few years after World War II. In 1947, Tanganyika was placed under the trusteeship of the United Nations (U.N.).

Under the U.N. trusteeship, Britain was given the task of developing Tanganyika's political scene. Britain supported the formation of the Tanganyika African National Union (TANU) in 1954, which was founded by Julius Nyerere. TANU candidates were successful in the Legislative Council elections of September 1958 and February 1959.

In December 1959, Britain approved a recommendation that moved Tanganyika toward self-government. In the 1960 elections, TANU representatives won a majority in the new government. In 1961, an independent Tanganyika emerged with Nyerere as its prime minister.

NYERERE: THE FATHER OF A NATION

Tanzania's first president, Julius Kambarage Nyerere, is well-loved among his country's people. Although some Tanzanians, looking back, view his bold ideas as failures, most remember him fondly as a leader who was honest, kind, and just.
(*A Closer Look, page 64*)

Zanzibar's Early Days

Zanzibar is an island that lies off the eastern coast of Tanganyika. The earliest inhabitants of Zanzibar were indigenous groups that had migrated from the African continent. Between the seventh and tenth centuries, Persians and Arabs settled in Zanzibar. They intermarried with the indigenous groups, and their descendents were known as Shirazis or Swahilis.

In 1503, the Portuguese forced Zanzibar to pay an annual tribute. Zanzibar continued to do so until 1698 when the Arabs expelled the Portuguese and regained control of the island. Under Arab ruler Seyyid Said bin Sultan (1806–1856), Zanzibar became an important center for commerce in East Africa and the Indian Ocean. At the same time, the slave market flourished, with Zanzibar at its center, until the slave trade was abolished in 1873.

Under the Treaty of Heligoland in 1890, Zanzibar was placed under British protection. A sultan remained in office on the island, but all decrees had to be approved by the British government. When the ruling sultan died in 1896, Khalid, a descendent of Seyyid Said, seized the throne. The British objected strongly to this and bombarded the palace. Khalid fled and took refuge with the Germans. The British then installed Hamud ibn Mohammed as the new sultan.

Above: **With Seyyid Said bin Sultan ruling the island, Zanzibar became an important commercial center in East Africa.**

Opposite: **Better known to locals as the Portuguese House, the Fukuchani ruins are still in good condition. The house was made out of coral bricks, and its design is believed to be Swahili in origin.**

12

In 1913, the British Colonial Office took over responsibility for Zanzibar and stationed a representative on the island. Executive and legislative councils were introduced in 1926 to help with the administration of Zanzibar.

In 1960, the British approved a new constitution for Zanzibar. Political parties emerged. One was the Zanzibar Nationalist Party (ZNP), which represented the Arab majority. Another was the Afro-Shirazi Party (ASP), which represented the African population.

In January 1961, the first Legislative Council elections were held, but the vote ended in a deadlock. In June of the same year, elections were held again. Amid riots and casualties, the ASP and ZNP won ten seats each, while the Zanzibar and Pemba People's Party (ZPPP) won three. The ZNP then joined forces with the ZPPP to form a majority government.

In December 1963, the British granted Zanzibar independence, and the island adopted a constitutional monarchy under a sultan for its government. A month later, the Africans of Zanzibar violently overthrew the sultan and formed a new government with Abeid Kurame, leader of the ASP, as president.

Above: **This building in Stone Town was once used as the headquarters of political parties.**

ZANZIBAR'S HOUSE OF WONDERS

Built in 1883, the House of Wonders was the most modern building in Zanzibar.
(*A Closer Look, page 72*)

THE ISLAND OF ZANZIBAR

Most people who travel to Zanzibar reach the island by ferry from Dar es Salaam or by airplane.
(*A Closer Look, page 56*)

13

Unification

In April 1964, Tanganyika and Zanzibar joined together to become the United Republic of Tanganyika and Zanzibar. Nyerere was installed as executive president and Kurame as first vice president. In October 1964, the Republic was renamed the United Republic of Tanzania.

Nyerere's policy of self-reliance and nationalization was outlined in the Arusha Declaration of 1967. This position was, however, not popular with the Tanzanian people. One of Nyerere's main political concerns was that Zanzibar's politics were in conflict with mainland Tanzania.

When Kurame was assassinated in 1972, Nyerere merged TANU and ASP to form the Revolutionary Party, or Chama Cha Mapinduzi (CCM), hoping that this would bring Zanzibar's political practices more in line with those of the mainland. The reverse, however, occurred — Zanzibar asked for more autonomy.

Nyerere resigned in 1985, and Ali Hassan Mwinyi took over as president. In order to revive the country's weak economy, Mwinyi accepted aid from the International Monetary Fund (IMF) and devalued Tanzania's currency. In 1992, the country's constitution was amended to allow for a multiparty government.

ARUSHA: CAPITAL OF EAST AFRICA

Tanzania's region of Arusha was formerly known as the Northern Region. It was established in 1963, and the city of Arusha is located in the central-eastern section of the region.
(A Closer Look, page 46)

FIGHTING IDI AMIN

In the late 1970s, President Julius Nyerere decided to provide military support to a group of Ugandan rebels that had been living in exile in Tanzania. Together, the Ugandan exiles and the Tanzanians entered Uganda and toppled notorious Ugandan dictator Idi Amin.
(A Closer Look, page 54)

Left: When Tanganyika and Zanzibar merged to become the United Republic of Tanzania, it was necessary to maintain the balance of power between the two previous regimes. This balance was attained with the appointment of Julius Nyerere (*right*) as executive president and Abeid Kurame (*left*) as first vice president.

Mirambo (1840–1884)

A warlord from central Africa, Mirambo united the various Nyamwezi clans into a mighty kingdom strong enough to prevent the Arabs from taking over the interior of Tanganyika. By employing the *ruga-ruga* (ROO-ga ROO-ga), who were paid warriors of the Ngoni people, and using firearms, he seized control of the major trade routes and made alliances with neighboring rulers. He established his capital at Urambo and turned it into a thriving commercial center. Mirambo's empire crumbled soon after his death, but he is remembered as a national hero.

Julius Nyerere

Julius Kambarage Nyerere (1922–1999)

Nyerere was the first Tanganyikan to be educated in Britain. He entered politics just as Britain was preparing Tanganyika for self-government. Nyerere formed the Tanganyika African National Union (TANU) in 1954. When an independent Tanganyika emerged in 1961, Neyerere was made prime minister. In 1962, he was elected president of the Republic of Tanganyika, and he retained his presidency when the United Republic of Tanzania formed in 1964. Nyerere was reelected for four consecutive terms until his resignation in 1985. During his presidency, Nyerere advocated a policy of self-sufficiency. He introduced *ujamaa* (OO-ja-MA-a), a form of collective farming, and policies that promoted education and literacy. In the 1970s, Nyerere clashed with Idi Amin, and in 1979, the Tanzanian army invaded Uganda to help topple Idi Amin.

Benjamin Mkapa

Benjamin William Mkapa (1938–)

First elected in 1995 and reelected in 2000, Mkapa is the current president of Tanzania. He was born in the southeastern region of Mtwara and educated in Tanganyika and Uganda. Mkapa's background in journlaism led to him being appointed press secretary for Julius Nyerere. In his political career, he has served as the high commissioner to Nigeria and Canada and as the ambassador to the United States. He has also held various positions in Tanzania's cabinet. Politically, Mkapa has always advocated democracy, trade, investment, and civil rights. He has also worked hard to fight poverty.

Government and Economy

The United Republic of Tanzania

The Tanzanian government consists of executive, legislative, and judicial branches. The executive branch is led by the president, who is also the head of state and the commander in chief of the armed forces of the country. The prime minister and cabinet ministers of Tanzania are chosen and appointed by the president from among the elected members of Tanzania's parliament. Each elected president serves a five-year term. Zanzibar elects its own president who heads a government for matters relating only to Zanzibar.

The legislative branch consists of a unicameral parliament called the National Assembly, or the *Bunge* (BUN-gay). The Bunge is made up of a total of 274 members, including 232 popularly elected representatives, thirty-seven women nominated by the president, and five members from the Zanzibar House of Representatives. All members serve five-year terms. The Zanzibar House of Representatives, which makes laws specifically for Zanzibar, consists of fifty popularly elected members, each of whom also serves a five-year term.

Opposite: **Supporters of the Chama Cha Mapinduzi (CCM), the political party to which President Benjamin Mkapa belongs, cheer in the streets.**

Left: **Voters cast ballots at one of the numerous polling stations during the 2000 election. In that election, Benjamin Mkapa was elected to office for a second term.**

Tanzania's judicial branch is based on the English common law system. It consists of district and primary courts, separate high courts for the Tanzanian mainland and Zanzibar, and the Court of Appeal for the United Republic. A high court consists of a head judge and twenty-nine judges who are appointed by the president. The Court of Appeal has a chief justice and four judges. The Permanent Commission of Enquiry investigates complaints against public officials.

Local Government

Tanzania is divided into twenty-five regions, twenty on the mainland and five on the islands. Each region is headed by a regional commissioner. The regions — Arusha, Dar es Salaam, Dodoma, Iringa, Kagera, Kigoma, Kilimanjaro, Lindi, Mara, Mbeya, Morogoro, Mtwara, Mwanza, Pemba North, Pemba South, Pwani, Rukwa, Ruvuma, Shinyanga, Singida, Tabora, Tanga, Zanzibar Central/South, Zanzibar North, and Zanzibar Urban/West — are further divided into 130 districts, which are headed by district commissioners.

THE UHURU TORCH

In 1961, Tanganyika was granted independence from British colonial rule. To mark the occasion, the Uhuru Torch was lit at the top of Mount Kilimanjaro. *Uhuru* (oo-HU-roo) means "freedom." The torch is a symbol of freedom and light for the Tanzanian people, and it is meant to bring hope, love, and respect in place of despair, enmity, and hatred. The Uhuru Torch Race is run annually and starts from a different place in Tanzania each time. The end of the race coincides with the public holiday named for the late president, Julius Nyerere.

Economy

Tanzania is one of the world's poorest countries, with more than one-third of the country's population living below the poverty line. Agriculture contributes greatly to Tanzania's economy. In 2001, the country's agricultural sector accounted for 48.1 percent of the country's gross domestic product (GDP), while the service sector accounted for 36.5 percent, and the industrial sector contributed the remaining 15.4 percent. Tanzania has a workforce of 13.5 million people. In 2002, Tanzania's agricultural sector employed 80 percent of the country's workforce. The remaining 20 percent worked in the industrial and service sectors.

In 2001, Tanzania purchased 13.3 percent of the country's imported goods from South Africa, 10.7 percent from Japan, 6.3 percent from the United Kingdom, and 6.2 percent from Kenya. Imported items included consumer goods, crude oil, equipment for machines and transportation, and industrial raw materials. In the same year, Tanzania exported cashew nuts, coffee, cotton, and gold. The three largest buyers of its products were India, Germany, and Belgium.

RESOURCES

Tanzania is rich in natural resources. Fish and prawns are caught in the country's many lakes. The country mines coal, diamonds, gold, kaolin, gypsum, nickel, tin, and a variety of gemstones, including tanzanite. Phosphate deposits and natural gas also exist in the country. The natural forests of Tanzania provide the raw materials for pulp and paper.

Below: In Tanzania, trains are important for transporting the country's exports.

Left: Sisal is one of the agricultural products that Tanzania exports. Sisal is processed to produce twine, which is also exported.

Agriculture

Most of the agricultural products grown in Tanzania are exported. They make up 85 percent of the products Tanzania sells to other countries. Coffee and cotton are two of the country's most important export cash crops. Cashew nuts, sisal, tea, and tobacco also account for a substantial amount of the cash crops that are exported. In certain areas, such as the Ruvuma and Rukwa regions, corn is also sold as a cash crop. Major food crops grown in Tanzania include bananas, barley, cassava, corn, millet, potatoes, rice, sorghum, sweet potatoes, and wheat. Zanzibar's main export is cloves. The island supplies 10 percent of the world's cloves.

Industry

The bulk of Tanzania's industrial sector thrives on the processing of locally produced agricultural goods. The industrial sector in Tanzania produces, among other items, sisal twine and sugar. Using materials bought from trade partners, Tanzania also manufactures cement, fertilizer, salt, shoes, textiles, and wood products. Tanzania also engages in mining activities and oil refining. Among some of the materials mined are diamonds, gold, and tanzanite.

Below: The island of Zanzibar is famous for the spices it exports, which include nutmeg.

THE ALLURE OF TANZANITE

Tanzanite, a rare and valuable mineral, was so named because Tanzania is the only country in the world where it has been found.

(A Closer Look, page 44)

People and Lifestyle

Ethnic Groups in Tanzania

In 2003, the population of Tanzania was almost 36 million, with Tanzanians between fifteen and sixty-four years old making up about 53 percent of the population. Slightly more than 44 percent are fourteen years old and younger, while just over 2 percent are sixty-five years and older. The number of men and women in Tanzania's population is fairly even, except among those sixty-five and older, where women outnumber men by more than 100,000.

Tanzania has more than 120 different ethnic groups, the majority of whom are descended from the Bantu, a large and diverse African linguistic group. The two largest of these groups are the Sukuma and the Nyamwezi. Despite their long histories, neither group has been dominant, culturally or politically.

Almost all Tanzanians living on the mainland are of native African descent, while minorities include Arabs, Asians, and Europeans. On Zanzibar, the ethnic mix is different. The Tanzanians living on the island of Zanzibar are of Arab, native African, or a combination of Arab and native African descent.

THE MAASAI

Famous for their colorful culture, the Maasai were once fiercely protective of their nomadic cattle-herding lifestyle. Twentieth-century developments, however, have forced more and more Maasai to abandon their traditional ways.
(A Closer Look, page 60)

Left: Tanzania's population is fairly young, with over 44 percent of the population fourteen years old or younger.

Rural and Urban Life

About 85 percent of Tanzania's people live a rural lifestyle. Traditionally, people have stayed in areas where the rainfall is lower because these are the places where tsetse flies are less likely to be a threat to humans. Most of the settlements that have sprung up are on the edges of the country: in the regions west and south of Lake Victoria, in the highland regions of Kilimanjaro and Mbeya, in the Mtwara area on the southern coast, and in the area around Dar es Salaam. Tanzanians living in rural areas have made their living from agriculture, using a system of crop rotation. As the rural population increased, land was farmed more intensely, causing the fertility of the soil to decline and harvests to suffer. When Julius Nyerere became president, he introduced the system of ujamaa. The policy failed because it forced many people to give up their lands and move to collective farms, an idea they did not like.

More than two million people — about one third of Tanzania's urban population — live in Dar es Salaam, the largest city. When the British were in control, Tanga was the second largest city because of its export of sisal. The city, however, is now the seventh largest, after Arusha, Mbeya, Mwanza, the city of Zanzibar, and Morogoro.

Above: **Over time, many indigenous peoples, such as the Maasai, have moved from their rural villages to cities in order to make better lives for themselves.**

UJAMAA

Ujamaa was a policy introduced under the Arusha Declaration of 1967. The main principles of the policy were to promote self-reliance and equal opportunity for all Tanzanians through collective production. Under the policy, farmers were reorganized into ujamaa villages. Each village specialized in one area of production.

Family Life

Families are important in Tanzanian society. Ties are strong between members of both immediate and extended families. Many of life's most important events, such as birth, death, puberty, and marriage, are celebrated on a large scale within family clans using traditional ceremonies. Disputes among family members are usually resolved by a panel consisting of clan members.

Men in Tanzania are traditionally allowed to take more than one wife. This trend is changing as more Tanzanians convert to Christianity. In recent times, many Muslim Tanzanians are also practicing monogamy.

While the men hunt and herd, the women work at household chores and the farming of crops. In rural families, children are looked at as assets, and having more children means that there are more people to help with the farming and herding. Girls are regarded as marriageable when they reach their early teens. Traditionally, marriages are arranged through a matchmaker, who could be a relative or a close friend of the family. Many ethnic groups still practice the controversial custom of paying a bride price.

PAYING A BRIDE PRICE

The custom of paying a bride price has a long history and is deeply rooted in Tanzanian culture. The practice continues even today.
(*A Closer Look, page 66*)

Opposite: Dispensaries provide basic health care to the rural population but can do little to change the unsanitary conditions of the rural areas. The result is a high infant mortality rate.

Below: Family still plays an important part in Tanzanian culture. For large families with two working parents, older siblings help look after the younger children.

Health

In 2003, it was estimated that Tanzanian women gave birth to an average of five to six children each. Tanzania's infant mortality rate, however, is high, since as many as 104 babies die at birth for every 1,000 born. Life expectancy is generally low. In 2003, it was estimated that Tanzanian men lived for an average of forty-three years, while the country's women outlived its men by almost three years.

In 1975, Tanzania's major health institutions were nationalized. The government introduced a health plan designed to provide basic health care to as many Tanzanians as possible. The national health policy of Tanzania places great emphasis on improving medical care for mothers and children, raising nutritional standards, and sanitation. The policy also aims to control the spread of communicable diseases, such as HIV/AIDS, and environmental diseases, such as malaria. A program to inoculate children has also been put into place.

Dispensaries serve most of the rural population, providing basic medical care and prescribing medication. Hospitals are found only in the country's urban areas.

CAUSES OF DEATH

Malaria causes most of the illnesses and deaths in Tanzania. Sleeping sickness is also widespread because the illness is transmitted by the tsetse fly, which is found in more than 60 percent of Tanzania. Where the population is dense, pneumonia becomes serious, since the rate of transmission by contact is high. In recent years, AIDS has contributed significantly to the mortality rate. In 2001, an estimated 7.8 percent of the adult population was infected with HIV.

Education

Tanzania's education system is divided into three stages — basic, secondary, and tertiary. Basic education incorporates two years of preprimary school and seven years of primary school. Secondary education consists of four years of junior secondary and two years of senior secondary school. At the tertiary stage, students can choose to attend a university, a university college, or a vocational training school.

Tanzania has one of the highest literacy rates in Africa, with more than 78 percent of the population ages fifteen and above being able to read and write either English, Swahili, or Arabic. This is the result of educational reforms that were put into place after the country became independent. Primary education was made mandatory. At the secondary level, emphasis was placed on practical subjects, such as agriculture, commerce, home economics, science, and technology. Another key feature of the education system is that what is taught at each level is complete in itself and not a continuation from one year to the next. Students participate in farming workshops to learn to apply basic agricultural methods and tools. Students are also taught

EQUAL OPPORTUNITY EDUCATION

Basic education in Tanzania is compulsory for both males and females, contributing to fairly high literacy rates for both genders. In 2003, almost 86 percent of the male population and just over 70 percent of the female population ages fifteen and above was literate. According to some reports, girls are less frequently enrolled in school than boys, even though basic edcation is mandatory.

about responsibility and cooperation through tasks and housekeeping chores. To bridge the gap between rural and urban, students in the towns are expected to work in nearby villages.

Higher Learning

By 2000, Tanzania had twenty-eight tertiary level institutions. Ten of these are universities, and they include the University of Dar es Salaam, Sokoine University of Agriculture, and Zanzibar University. There are seven university colleges, among which are the Kilimanjaro Christian Medical Center, University College of Lands and Architectural Studies, and the College of Education Zanzibar. There are also eleven nonuniversity vocational training schools, or specialty institutions, such as the College of Business Education, the Tanzania School of Journalism, and the Dar es Salaam Institute of Technology.

Adult education is important and the Tanzanian government has introduced programs aimed at making adults more aware of certain areas of knowledge, such as agricultural methods, crafts, hygiene, and mathematics.

Left: Tanzania's school curriculum teaches practical subjects, such as agriculture and commerce, that students are able to apply to everyday life.

Religion

In Tanzania, 35 percent of the people on the mainland and 99 percent of the people on the neighboring islands practice Islam. About 30 percent of mainland Tanzanians identify themselves as Christians, and 35 percent hold indigenous beliefs. In practice, however, many Tanzanians living in the rural areas combine elements of indigenous beliefs with Islam or Christianity. Small numbers of people within the Asian minorities practice Buddhism, Hinduism, and Sikhism. The Baha'i faith also has some followers in the country.

Islam

Islam was first introduced to Zanzibar when the Arabs built trading posts on the island. From there, the religion spread to the mainland as the Arabs moved inland in search of more items to trade. Today, Muslims can be found living in or near Dar es Salaam, Kigoma, Kondoa, Singida, Tabora, and Tanga. A large population of Muslims is present in the towns that have sprung up along the Ruvuma River. Almost all the Tanzanians living on Pemba and Zanzibar Islands follow the Islamic faith. Muslim

THE RELIGIONS OF THE LUGURU

The Luguru are a Bantu-speaking people who reside in the Uluguru Mountains and the surrounding coastal plains. Those living in the mountain region are mainly Roman Catholic, while those in the lowland areas are Muslim.

Below: **Arabs brought the Islamic faith when they settled on the island of Zanzibar. Mosques have separate areas for men and women.**

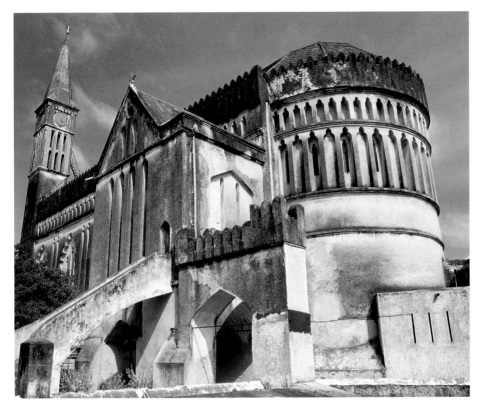

Left: **The Church of Christ in the city of Zanzibar was the first Anglican cathedral in East Africa. Built in the 1870s, the church stands on the site of the old slave market. The constitution of Tanzania allows for religious freedom. Tanzanian Christians consist of Protestants, Roman Catholics, Pentecostals, Mormons, Jehovah's Witnesses, and Seventh-Day Adventists. Foreign missionaries are found, including those from Lutheran, Anglican, Catholic, Mormon, and Baptist denominations.**

affairs in Tanzania are handled on the mainland by the National Muslim Council of Tanzania and on the islands by the Supreme Muslim Council.

Christianity

When the Portuguese were in Tanganyika, Roman Catholic Franciscans set up a mission at Kilwa. This was the first contact the country had with Christianity. During the British colonial period, more missions were established by the various Christian denominations. Many of these denominations are still present in Tanzania today. Lutherans and Roman Catholics are Tanzania's largest Christian groups. The Christian Council of Tanzania oversees all the affairs of the various denominations.

Indigenous Beliefs

Many indigenous religions are present in Tanzania, most of which have a higher being as a central figure. Belief in ancestral spirits is strong, and it is not uncommon to find a child with a Christian or Muslim first name coupled with an ethnic middle name that once belonged to an ancestor.

Language and Literature

Also known as Kiswahili, Swahili is one of at least eighty-seven languages spoken in Tanzania. Swahili is the official national language and is spoken by almost all Tanzanians. Swahili is used by the country's government and is also used during the first seven years of school. English is the country's second official language. It is used for commerce and higher education.

Swahili is a Bantu language that has been influenced by Arabic. The name *Swahili* comes from the Arabic word *sawahili*, which means "of the coast." The language contains many Arabic words because of the contact between Arab traders and coastal Africans over many centuries. The form of Swahili used today is called Standard Swahili. It is derived from Kiunguja, a Swahili dialect spoken by the people of Zanzibar and coastal Tanzania.

Many Tanzanians, especially those in Zanzibar, also speak Arabic. Others mainly speak local languages. Swahili itself has fifteen dialects and various pidgin forms.

Below: **It is not uncommon to find a mixture of English and Swahili in educational materials in Tanzania.**

Tanzanian Literature

Tanzania has a rich oral tradition. Stories have been passed down from one generation to the next. Printed Tanzanian literature began in the 1930s, when the British colonists adopted Swahili as a language for education and publishing. Early fiction in Swahili was inspired by Tanzania's oral tradition. Other fiction available in Swahili consists of translated stories written by European authors. Today, the most popular stories in Tanzania deal with romance, intrigue, and mystery. Historical writing is also popular. Most recently, Tanzanians have produced works of literary criticism as well as Swahili translations of works of African authors from other countries.

One of the most outstanding Tanzanian literary figures is Shaaban Robert (1909–1962). Robert strongly promoted Swahili culture and the African oral tradition. His works, which include novels, poems, and essays, gained popularity between the 1940s and the 1960s. Muhammed Saleh Farsy and Muhammed Said Abdulla, both from Zanzibar, are other Tanzanian authors who became known during this era. Tanzanian authors today who have received international recognition include Euphrase Kezilahabi, Mohammed S. Mohammed, and Tololwa Mollel.

Arts

Musical Instruments

Historically, Tanzanians used drums to herald the arrival or departure of leaders, keep rhythm, and build morale. Certain drums were also used to summon villagers or call them to battle. Tanzanian drums come in different shapes and sizes. These include small drums that are held between the knees, large drums that have specially constructed supports, and drums that have pointed bases that are pushed into the ground for support. In Tanzania, the *marimba* (ma-RIM-ba), a finger piano that consists of a range of metal springs of varying lengths that resonate against a wooden box, is a common instrument. The Tanzanian guitar is a large violin-like instrument fitted with a coconut shell resonator.

Above: **Beaded clubs made by the Maasai people are part of Tanzania's rich arts heritage.**

Dance and Music

In Tanzania, the dances of indigenous groups express many emotions. The *ngoma* (ng-OH-ma) is a traditional dance and

musical form used to depict everyday life, celebrate special occasions, or uphold traditions. Styles of dancing vary from one tribal group to another. The Maasai leap in the air and chant, the Makonde shake their bottoms, the Sukuma hold live snakes, and the Zaramo move in an undulating procession.

The *chakacha* (cha-KA-cha) and the *lelemama* (LEH-leh-MA-ma) are two traditional Tanzanian dances performed solely by women. The chakacha looks similar to belly dancing. In the lelemama, women make complicated hand movements. These dances are popular in Tanzania's coastal areas and islands, and they are usually performed at weddings.

In Zanzibar, *taarab* (taa-RAB) is a common musical form in which poetry is sung. It was introduced to the islands by Sultan Seyyid Barghash, and Arabic was the primary language sung. In 1928, however, Siti bint Saad began singing the taarab in her native Swahili, starting a new trend. Even after her death in 1950, this tradition continued. The taarab is commonly known as "Swahili wedding music." Other musical forms in Tanzania include the dance music known both as *mtindo* (mu-EEN-doh) and "urban jazz."

Above: Dance is very much a part of tribal life. The indigenous peoples of Tanzania each have their own dance traditions.

Opposite: The Dar es Salaam Music and Dance Festival (left) is a competition in which people from the different areas of mainland Tanzania perform ethnic dances and music. At the Zanzibar Cultural Festival, traditional dances and music such as taarab are featured alongside art and crafts.

31

Handicrafts

Tanzania's different indigenous groups are known for different artistic skills. The skills of the Makonde and the Maasai are among the most well known. The Makonde are renowned for their wood carving skills, which they demonstrate on the masks and figurines that they create. The Maasai produce stunning designs on their shields and spears. They have also gained fame for incorporating beads into their ceremonial collars and other everyday objects, making them works of art.

Tanzanians make handwoven baskets that have geometric patterns. The baskets are made from bamboo leaves, palm leaves, or different types of grass, which are dyed to produce a wide range of colors. Over time, the quality of the dyes has improved, and the colors of the baskets have become more vibrant. Along the coast, handwoven mats are made of the same materials. These mats are used for sleeping, sitting, and drying food items. Some are used as prayer mats in places of worship.These mats sometimes have verses from the Qur'an or praises to the Islamic god, Allah, written on them. Tanzanians also use the same materials and weaving methods to create trays and decorative items.

MAKONDE WOOD CARVINGS

The wood carvings of the Makonde are known by people all over the world. Most of their carvings are made out of ebony, one of the hardest woods in the world.
(A Closer Look, page 62)

Tanzanians have made pots for about one thousand years. Clay pots were made and used for cooking and holding water. Today, Tanzanians still make pots using traditional methods. The most beautiful ones are created by the elderly women of the villages. The quality of a pot depends on the type of clay out of which it is made and how it is fired. Some of the most durable pots are made from clay taken from Mount Kilimanjaro and the Pare Mountains.

Zanzibar's Carved Doors

Zanzibar is renowned for its unique doors, which have been carved with elaborate designs that reflect the island's Arabic heritage. This art form became especially popular in the 1800s when craftsmen combined elements from the indigenous Swahili culture with elements from the Islamic tradition. In the past, the door was the first part of the house to be created and installed. The size and intricacy of the design on the door often reflected the social status and wealth of the owner of the house. Many Zanzibari doors have decorative studs or spikes. The oldest door in Zanzibar is said to date back to 1694, and there are about 560 carved doors on the island at last count.

TINGATINGA ART

Tingatinga is a Tanzanian style of painting that was pioneered by Edward Saidi Tingatinga. Even though his body of work was limited, he has left a legacy that has inspired many followers who produce a distinctive art form that is now known by people worldwide.
(A Closer Look, page 68)

Below: **The** *dhow* **(DA-ow) is a typical Tanzanian boat, and people not only make life-size dhows but also carve miniatures to sell as souvenirs.**

Leisure and Festivals

Popular Pastimes

In their spare time, Tanzanians like to sing and dance, socialize, visit with friends and relatives, tell stories, play games, and participate in sports activities.

Storytelling is an effective way to have fun and entertain friends. The Tanzanian storytelling tradition also provides a means for transmitting social and cultural values, teaching the young about the rules of society, and reinforcing its framework and boundaries to adults.

Some popular stories in Tanzanian folklore concern Kibo and Mawenzi, two of the peaks of Mount Kilimanjaro. In one story, Kibo and Mawenzi were brothers. One day, the two were smoking their pipes when Mawenzi's pipe went out. Mawenzi used Kibo's fire to relight his pipe, but it went out again after Mawenzi fell asleep. Mawenzi asked Kibo for the same favor again. The irritated Kibo hit his brother until Mawenzi's face was damaged. Ever since, Mawenzi has hidden behind the clouds. The story is said to explain why the peak of Mawenzi is more rugged-looking than Kibo and is usually surrounded by clouds.

Left: The social life and recreational acivities of Tanzanians revolve around the family. In their free time, they will visit relatives and friends, gather at each other's homes, or meet at a roadside stall to chat and drink beverages.

ORAL CULTURE

Storytelling in Tanzania is part of a larger oral culture that includes riddles, proverbs, myths, legends, and folklore.

Bao

Bao (BA-ow) is a popular board game among Tanzanians. Bao and its variations are believed to have developed about three thousand years ago in Africa or Asia, where they are still played to this day. Bao boards may range from a simple plank of wood to an elaborate piece that has been decorated with stylized shapes and carvings.

The typical bao board has four rows of hollow pits carved into it. The two rows nearest each player belong to that player. Before the game starts, some of the pits in each front row are filled with a certain number of seeds. Each player will also have a stock of seeds on the side. In each turn, players take one seed from their stock and place it in one of their own front pits that is facing an occupied pit belonging to the opponent. The seeds in that occupied pit will now belong to the player who made the move.

The object of the game is to win as many of your opponent's seeds as possible. A player does this by making sure that there are no seeds in the opponent's front row or by strategically preventing the opponent from making an allowed move.

Above: In Tanzania, the wooden bao board has four rows of eight pits each. Two of the pits are square or rectangular instead of round.

BAO BOOK

Bao has intrigued minds beyond the borders of Africa. Alexander de Voogt of Leiden University in the Netherlands wrote a book titled *Mancala Board Games* in 1997 after studying bao masters at tournaments.

Sports

Tanzanians love to play soccer. Barefoot children can be seen playing soccer in the streets and on fields, using homemade balls made of plastic bags wrapped and tied together. The country's national soccer team is the Taifa Stars. Though professional soccer is popular in Tanzania, it suffers from corrupt leadership and players who are not world-class athletes.

Tanzanian women and girls like to play netball. Netball is a sport played by two opposing teams of seven players each. The object of the game is to throw the ball into the net and score as many goals as possible. The game is similar to basketball. In netball, however, the player who holds the ball must keep at least one foot on the ground. The player also cannot dribble the ball or hold it for more than three seconds. The Tanzania Netball Association is the governing body for the sport in the country.

In Tanzania, running is also a popular sport. Marathons are held regularly. Since 1985, the country has held the Mount Meru International Marathon annually to discover and nurture good

Above: **Children in Tanzania make soccer balls out of plastic bags.**

CECAFA

The Council for East and Central Africa Football Association (CECAFA) is made up of eleven countries, one of which is Tanzania. The association holds the CECAFA Senior Challenge Cup every year. Tanzania reached the finals of the tournament in 2002 but lost to Kenya.

Left: **Tanzanians enjoy playing soccer. The national team, the Taifa Stars, has taken part in the African Cup of Nations competition.**

runners. Young people between the ages of thirteen and seventeen can take part in a junior version of the marathon. The Kilimanjaro Marathon, which was first held in 2003, is a gruelling 26-mile (42-km) run over different types of terrain.

Several Tanzanian runners, such as Francis Naali, John Yuda, and Filbert Bayi, have won medals in world competitions. Naali won a gold medal for the men's marathon at the 2002 Commonwealth Games, while Yuda clinched a bronze medal for the 6-mile (10,000-meter) run at the same competition. Bayi broke the world record for the 1,500-meter run during the 1974 Commonwealth Games. In 1975, he set another world record for his one-mile run in Jamaica.

Other popular sports in Tanzania are boxing and rugby. There are a number of rugby teams across the country, including the Arusha Rhinos. Boxing is another sport in which Tanzanians have excelled. One of the biggest names is Rashid Matumla, who, in 1998, became the first Tanzanian to win the World Boxing Union title for the light-middleweight category.

Above: **In the 1998 Commonwealth Games held in Malaysia, Michael Yomba (*left*) of Tanzania defeated Clied Musonda (*right*) of Zimbabwe during the quarter-final match in the bantamweight category. Yomba made it through to the semifinals and eventually won the gold medal.**

Idd-El-Fitr and Idd-El-Hajj

Thirty-five percent of the people on mainland Tanzania and almost everyone on the nearby islands are Muslims. Because of this, the Islamic festivals of *Idd-El-Fitr* (EAD-al-FIT-er) and *Idd-El-Hajj* (EAD-al-HAJ) are celebrated with great cheer.

During Ramadan, the ninth month in the Islamic calendar, Muslims fast from sunrise to sunset. Shops and restaurants remain closed during the day and open only after dusk. Idd-El-Fitr marks the end of Ramadan. Tanzanians celebrate this festival by preparing a feast for friends and relatives and by buying and wearing new clothes. Men from certain parts of Zanzibar have a tradition of hitting each other lightly with branches from banana trees to celebrate Idd-El-Fitr. The women enliven the celebration by singing songs.

During Idd-El-Hajj, Tanzanian Muslims who can afford the trip perform a pilgrimage to Mecca in Saudi Arabia. Tanzanian Muslims also slaughter goats during this festival.

Above: **Although Islam is the main religion on the island of Zanzibar, some Hindus also live on the island. Krishna is one of the most important gods in Hinduism. To celebrate Krishna's birthday, one of the main festivals on the Hindu calendar, these Zanzibari Hindus gather together.**

Other Festivals

Tanzanians celebrate Independence Day on December 9. The holiday marks Tanganyika's independence from Britain in 1961 and Zanzibar's independence in 1963. The day is a national holiday. Tanzanians celebrate Independence Day with activities such as watching military parades. The Uhuru Torch race was introduced in 1961 to mark Tanganyika's independence from colonial rule. The tradition was started by Julius Nyerere, who lit the first torch on Mount Kilimanjaro. The race starts from several different places in Tanzania and is timed to end on the anniversary of Nyerere's death.

The annual Festival of the Dhow Countries takes place in Zanzibar, and it consists of cultural and artistic events and dhow races. The term "dhow countries" refers to Africa, the Gulf states, Iran, the Indian subcontinent, and the Indian Ocean islands.

During Christmas, Tanzanian Christians, like most Christians around the world, exchange presents and take part in church services. One important part of the Christmas celebration in Tanzania is spending time with one's family.

Below: July 7 is Saba Saba, a holiday that celebrates the founding of the Tanganyika African National Union (TANU) in 1954 by Julius Nyerere. Saba Saba was called Peasant's Day but is now renamed International Trade Fair.

Food

In much of Tanzania, the staple food is *ugali* (u-GA-lih). This is a dough-like porridge made from cassava, cornmeal, millet, or sorghum. Ugali is generally eaten with meat, stew, or vegetables. In the coastal regions, the staple food is pilaf, which is rice seasoned with pepper, cinnamon, cumin, or curry. The favorite meats of the Tanzanians are chicken, goat, beef, and mutton.

In Tanzania, one popular dish is *mishikaki* (mih-shih-KA-kih), which is meat that has been broiled over a charcoal fire. Duckling Dar-es-Salaam is considered a delicacy in the country and is usually served when special guests are present. A favorite snack among Tanzanians is *maandazi* (man-DA-zee), which is a sweet fried bread that is similar to a doughnut. Other snacks that Tanzanians enjoy are chapatis, peanuts, samosas, and sugar cane. Plantains are commonly eaten in the northern and southern highlands and in the area around Lake Victoria. On the islands, near rivers and lakes, and along the coastal regions, seafood is easily available. In Zanzibar, curries, fish, and grilled octopus are among the foods enjoyed by Tanzanians.

Left: **Women in the city of Arusha prepare dough to make bread.**

Above: **Fruit markets can be found on the island of Zanzibar.**

On the mainland, hot tea is a popular beverage among Tanzanians, especially when they are socializing. In Zanzibar, sugar cane juice is a popular drink. Desserts in Tanzania usually include the fresh fruit available in the country's various regions.

Eating Etiquette

In Tanzania, it is common to eat with your hands. A bowl of water is usually passed around before and after the meal for the washing of hands. It is also common to eat from a communal bowl. The proper custom for eating in this way is to use only your right hand when putting food into your mouth or selecting food from the common bowl. The left hand should only be used to handle difficult-to-handle items like pieces of meat with bones.

In Tanzania, different cultural groups have different mealtime customs and dietary restrictions. Some indigenous groups ban men from entering the kitchen, while others do not allow fathers-in-law to eat together with their daughters-in-law. Some women in certain indigenous groups do not eat any chicken or eggs. In certain Muslim households, the dining areas for men and women are separate. Some families sit on woven mats placed on the floor while they eat their meals.

A CLOSER LOOK AT TANZANIA

The United Republic of Tanzania may have existed for only about forty years, but the country possesses a prehistory that dates back to the dawn of human life. Colonization by various European and Arab powers has have left a mark not just on the politics and culture of the country, but also on its architecture and religion.

Some indigenous groups, however, have clung staunchly to their own beliefs and way of life. These groups, with their wealth of cultural traditions, make up a unique Tanzanian mosaic. Some of these groups, such as the Makonde, are renowned for their artistic skills and have made a name for themselves worldwide.

Opposite: **The Maasai are a seminomadic people who measure their wealth in cattle.**

Tanzanians are a sociable people with a strong community spirit. They usually celebrate special occasions among their extended families. Their storytelling tradition not only educates the young, but also reinforces societal values among adults.

From the heights of Mount Kilimanjaro to the plains of the Serengeti and from the exotic beauty of the Zanzibar Islands to the ruggedness of the Selous Game Reserve, Tanzania is home to many natural wonders and historical sites. The country's natural resources and the creations of its indigenous peoples have helped to raise its status on the international scene.

Above: **Stone Town, located on the island of Zanzibar, was named a UNESCO World Heritage site in 2000. Many old buildings in the town are still intact, and they reflect the cultural heritage of the island.**

The Allure of Tanzanite

A Unique Gemstone

Tanzania is the only country in the world where tanzanite, a rare and sought-after mineral, is mined. Because of its distinctive color, which consists of blended shades of dark blue and purple, tanzanite is commonly used as a gemstone in expensive jewelry.

Technically, tanzanite is a colored crystal and a semiprecious mineral. Its extreme rarity, howver, has made it as valuable as precious stones. Tanzanite is part of the zoisite family of minerals and it is scientifically known as hydrous calcium aluminum silicate.

Tanzanite measures between six and seven on the Moh's scale, which is used to measure minerals for their hardness and susceptibility to scratches. Diamond measures ten, which is the highest end of the scale, making it the hardest and most scratch-resistant of all minerals. Because pieces of tanzanite fracture or crack easily, they have to be handled with extreme care during cleaning and cutting.

Left: **Although tanzanite is known to occur in other colors, such as green, yellowish-brown, or reddish-purple, the dark blue variety is the most prized.**

A Worldwide Sensation

Tanzanite was first discovered in 1967. Some Maasai herdsmen reportedly saw some objects glistening in the sun when they traveled past the plains near Mount Kilimanjaro and picked them up. Since then, more tanzanite has been mined from the Merelani hills, near the city of Arusha, and presented to experts around the world. Nicknamed the "gemstone of the twentieth century," tanzanite became one of the most sought-after gemstones for jewelry, especially after a world-renowned jewelry company, Tiffany of New York, promoted it with an advertising campaign in 1969. One of the more spectacular specimens of tanzanite known to the world is kept in the National Museum of Natural History in Washington, D.C. On display in the museum is a piece of tanzanite, called "The Midnight Blue," that weighs a staggering 122.7 carats. Precious and semiprecious stones are measured in carats, and a carat is approximately 200 milligrams.

Unlike the diamond trade in some African nations, the tanzanite industry enjoys a good reputation around the world. Estimates suggest that about 90 percent of the world's tanzanite traders are members of the International Colored Gemstone Association (ICA), an organization that ensures ethical standards are met in the acquiring and treating of gemstones.

TERRORISM AND TANZANITE

In November 2001, U.S. companies began a short-lived boycott of tanzanite following reports suggesting that members of the al-Qaeda network — the group responsible for numerous terrorist attacks around the world, including the September 11, 2001, attacks in the United States — were smuggling tanzanite to help raise funds for the group's activities. No convincing evidence supported this claim, however, and by August 2002, U.S. jewelry companies, including Tiffany and Zale, of Texas, were again buying tanzanite.

Arusha: Capital of East Africa

Perched at 5,053 feet (1,540 m) above sea level, the city of Arusha is located in the region of the same name. The region of Arusha covers an area of about 33,240 square miles (86,100 square km). In 2002, it is estimated that the city of Arusha had a population of about 2.7 million people.

The Regional Capital

Arusha has a reputation for being an important city because it is the seat of several intergovernmental and international organizations. Kenya, Tanzania, and Uganda — each of which shares a border with the others — have shared diplomatic ties and cooperative law enforcement policies since 1927. Over several decades, this alliance developed into the East African Community (EAC). Arusha has hosted a number of EAC summits, and in November 2001, during the third EAC summit held in Arusha, two additional intergovernmental bodies — the East African Legislative Assembly and the East African Court of Justice — were officially opened. Both offices are based in Arusha.

Opposite: **The Meru Crater lies within the Arusha National Park. Although Meru has had four previous eruptions, the volcano is currently dormant.**

DECADES OF FRIENDSHIP

Over the years, diplomatic ties between Kenya, Uganda, and Tanzania were fostered by several organizations: the East African High Commission (1948–1961), the East African Common Services Organization (1961–1967), the East African Community (EAC) (1967–1977), and the East African Co-operation (1993–2000). In 1999, the three countries decided to reform the EAC and signed a treaty in Arusha. That treaty took effect in July 2000.

Left: **The Arusha International Conference Center has conference facilities, exhibition halls, and seminar rooms. The center also has a restaurant and food services, recreational facilities, medical services, communication services, and a shopping arcade.**

Outside of East African political organizations, embassies of Denmark, France, Italy, and the United Kingdom and offices of nongovernmental organizations (NGOs), including World Vision International and Oxfam International, are present in Arusha. Also located in Arusha is the International Criminal Tribunal for Rwanda. The tribunal was created by a United Nations Security Council resolution. It was established so that leaders of the 1994 genocide in Rwanda could be brought to justice.

The Crossroads of East Africa

In the city of Arusha stands a tower that marks the halfway point between Cairo, Egypt, and Cape Town, South Africa. Also known as the Arusha Airport, the Kilimanjaro International Airport is used by most travelers to the region, especially government officials and tourists. Because the airport is located in Arusha, many tourists use the city as a base for exploring the surrounding natural wonders, including the Serengeti region, the Ngorongoro Crater, Olduvai Gorge, and Mount Kilimanjaro. For government officials and working professionals, regular flights connect Arusha and Johannesburg, the capital of South Africa, while daily flights operate between Arusha and Nairobi, the capital of neighboring Kenya. Although the airport is modest in size, it can accommodate airplanes as big as Boeing 747s.

ARUSHA NATIONAL PARK

Called a "little gem" by some, Arusha National Park is located about 20 miles (32 km) away from the city of Arusha and has an area of about 53 square miles (137 square km). The park is appropriately nicknamed considering the region's heavyweights, including Lake Manyara, Mount Kilimanjaro, Serengeti, and Tarangire National Parks. Nevertheless, Arusha National Park is famous for its diverse landscapes — including the Meru Crater, the Momella Lakes, and the Ngurdoto Crater — and rich animal life. Giraffes, hippopotamuses, hyenas, elephants, and baboons are found in the park, and bird life is rich there.

47

Bagamoyo's Slave Trade

A sleepy seaside town, Bagamoyo is located 45 miles (75 km) north of Dar es Salaam and looks onto the waters of the Zanzibar Channel. Life in Bagamoyo, however, was very different back in the eighteenth and nineteenth centuries, when it crawled with activity as one of East Africa's largest slave-trading centers.

The Name Says It All

According to many accounts, Bagamoyo's name is a reminder of the role the town played in the slave trade. Although people have argued about the meaning of "Bagamoyo," many believe that the word is Swahili for "crush down your heart" or "lay down your heart." It is believed that the slaves, before boarding ships at Bagamoyo that took them to faraway lands, shared the general feeling of wanting to leave their hearts behind on African soil. From the town of Ujiji — which lies on the eastern coast of Lake Tanganyika, at the other end of the slave route — slaves and their captors then journeyed on foot for about 932 miles (1,500 km), over punishing terrain.

Left: This illustration shows an artist's idea of what Bagamoyo may have looked like in the eighteenth and nineteenth centuries. In 2002, it was estimated that more than 41,150 Tanzanians were living in the city of Bagamoyo.

Left: Slaves were often treated like animals. They were held with chains and manacles in dark and damp quarters and were given little food and water.

The Slave Traders

The Omani Arabs were the main players in the region's slave trade. In fact, Omani monarch Seyyid Said bin Sultan, who transferred the capital of Oman from Muscat to Zanzibar in 1832, vigorously supported the expansion of the region's slave trade. So lucrative was the business that many slave dealers — with no regard for human suffering — sought to enslave more people. Some turned to kidnapping, while others persuaded tribal chiefs to sell their subjects. Some slave dealers even went as far as to incite tribal conflicts to advance their trade. By inciting conflict, the slave dealers stood to gain because the tribes involved in the conflicts would capture members of opposing tribes, and these prisoners would be more readily sold by their captors than by chiefs of their own groups.

Some accounts of the appalling conditions in which the slaves were held describe them being chained together by the neck or held in pens, like farm animals. In the mid-nineteenth century, renowned scientist and explorer Dr. David Livingstone began a mission to document and expose the ills and injustices of the slave trade in the interior regions. He observed that ten slaves died for every one slave that survived the ordeal of walking from the interior to the coast. The Zanzibar slave market formally closed in 1873, but the slave trade in the region continued until Dar es Salaam became the new center for trade and commerce.

THE FIRST CAPITAL OF TANGANYIKA

In 1887, the German East Africa Company declared Bagamoyo the capital of Tanganyika. Bagamoyo operated as the capital of the land for four years. In 1891, Dar es Salaam replaced Bagamoyo as the capital.

Endangered Elephants

Established in 1975, the Convention on International Trade in Endangered Species of Wild Fauna and Flora (CITES) seeks to protect, among other species, elephants around the world from indiscriminate hunting. Only two species of elephants exist in the world — the Asian elephant (*Elephas maximus*) and the African elephant (*Loxodonta africana*). Many African nations, including Tanzania, became members of CITES in the 1980s. Since 1989, CITES has banned members from participating in the trade of ivory or ivory products, which come from elephant tusks.

Killed for Their Tusks

Although the international ivory trade had been steadily increasing since the 1940s, the rapid slaughter of African elephants for their tusks began only in the 1970s. At that time, automatic weapons were freely available, and many ivory-exporting countries had corrupt government officials who did little to stop poachers from killing the elephants in their countries. By the 1980s, the elephant populations in some African nations, including Tanzania, were seriously threatened. By 1989, Tanzania was reportedly losing up to 16 percent of the country's elephants annually.

CONFISCATED IVORY

In 2003, Tanzania sought permission from CITES to sell the stock of ivory that it held in government warehouses. About 88,183 tons (80,000 tonnes) of tusks had been either seized from poachers over the years or removed from elephants that died of natural causes. Tanzanian authorities are hoping to advance the country's development with the money earned from the sale of this ivory.

Some countries, such as Botswana, Namibia and South Africa, already have permission to sell the ivory that they have confiscated.

Left: **Poverty prompted some people to kill elephants. From the 1970s to the 1980s, the price of ivory rose by 150 percent, from U.S. $50 to U.S. $125 for every pound (0.45 kilogram).**

Efforts to Save the Elephants

Uhai is a Swahili word for "life."Launched in 1989, Operation Uhai was a campaign aimed at protecting certain native animal species, including elephants, from poachers operating in the Selous Game Reserve. The reserve is the second-largest in Africa and home to the largest population of elephants in Tanzania. According to figures from the Tanzanian Wildlife Research Institute (TAWIRI), about 60,000 elephants roamed the reserve in 1999, compared to 35,000 in 1990.

In the Serengeti National Park, more than 4,300 poachers were arrested by Tanzanian authorities between the mid- and the late 1990s. The tools the poachers used to sustain their trade, including guns, machetes, and hunting dogs, were confiscated. Although poachers are still known to operate in twenty-first-century Tanzania, the country's wildlife authorities have been working hard to defeat them. Among the actions that the authorities have taken include training their staffs to overcome increasingly sophisticated poaching weapons and techniques and gaining the support of Tanzanians to report any poacher they see.

Above: **Ivory is often used to produce sculptures, bracelets, necklaces and other small souvenir items.**

Exploring the Olduvai Gorge

Part of the Ngorongoro Conservation Area, the Olduvai Gorge is an important archaeological site. Geographically, the gorge is better described as a ravine, or a narrow, steep-sided valley created by running water that eroded land over thousands of years. The Olduvai Gorge measures about 30 miles (48 km) long and about 295 feet (90 m) deep. Tests performed on the exposed rock surfaces on either side of the gorge show that some parts are more than two million years old.

Seven Beds

The Olduvai Gorge includes seven main formations, or fossil beds. Materials from the first bed, or Bed I, are the oldest, at between 1.7 and 2.1 million years old. Bed II ranges from about 1.2 to 1.7 million years old, and Bed III from 800,000 to about 1.2 million years. Bed IV is said to be between 600,000 and 800,000 years in age. The remaining beds are the Masek Beds (400,000 to 600,000 years old), the Ndutu Beds (32,000 to 400,000 years old), and the Naisiusiu Beds (15,000 to 22,000 years old).

Opposite: **The Olduvai Museum houses various fossils that have been discovered over the years in the gorge.**

Below: **More than fifty hominid fossils were discovered at the Olduvai Gorge. The gorge is part of a World Heritage site selected by UNESCO in 1979.**

Peeks into Prehistory

In 1959, renowned archaeologists Louis (1903–1972) and Mary (1913–1996) Leakey announced a momentous discovery they made in Bed I. Mary Leakey had unearthed the skull of a hominid. Although Louis Leaky believed the skull was an example of the species *Zinjanthropus boisei*, later research showed that it was more accurately classed as *Australopithecus boisei*. To most people, it is known as the "Nutcracker Man," a hominid who is believed to have lived some 1.75 million years ago.

Numerous important archaeological discoveries supporting the theory of evolution have been made in Bed II. The remains of *Homo habilis,* believed to be the first human ancestor that used tools, were unearthed in the 1960s from the lower section of Bed II, and the skull of a *Homo erectus* was found near the top of Bed II. Evidence of *Australopithecus boisei* has also been discovered throughout Bed II.

Tools from the Stone Age have been found in Beds III and IV. According to Mary Leakey, the Olduvai Gorge was the site of three eras of early human tool use — the Oldowan, the Developed Oldowan, and the Early Acheulean.

DISCOVERING TEETH

Four years before the Leakeys made their major discovery of the *Australopithecus boisei* skull, Louis Leakey unearthed two hominid baby teeth in the Olduvai Gorge.

FINDING FOOTPRINTS

Mary Leakey made a fantastic discovery at Laetoli, a site about 30 miles (48 km) south of the Olduvai Gorge. At this site, she found perfectly preserved footprints made by a hominid about three million years ago.

Fighting Idi Amin

The Tyrant Next Door

Idi Amin (c. 1925–2003) was a career soldier from Tanzania's neighbor, Uganda, who rose through the ranks of the British colonial army and became a regionally feared dictator for much of the 1970s. In January 1971, while Milton Obote (1924–), Uganda's president, was attending a conference in Singapore for British Commonwealth nations, Amin staged a military coup and shortly after declared himself the president of Uganda and the chief of its armed forces. Tanzania, under the leadership of Julius Nyerere, offered Obote refuge upon his return to Africa.

Amin ruled Uganda from 1971 to 1979. In 1972, Obote, while living in exile in Tanzania, attempted to regain control of Uganda by calling on his supporters in the Ugandan army to rise up and fight Amin. Obote's plan failed, leading to ethnic division and discrimination in Uganda and cross-border attacks on villages

Below: **Idi Amin led Uganda for only eight years. In that time, he made a number of radical political moves, both domestically and internationally, that left Uganda in utter disarray. He was toppled from power in 1979.**

in Tanzania. Because Obote was Lango and most of the Ugandan soldiers who supported him were Acholi, Amin, who was Kakwa, ordered that every Acholi and Lango person in the Ugandan army be removed. The mood of Amin's "cleanup operation" then spread to Ugandan civilians. The result was that thousands of Acholi and Lango people were persecuted. Tanzania opened its doors to Ugandan refugees and exiles from Amin's regime.

The Beginning of the End

In October 1978, Amin, whose grip on power in Uganda had ruined the country politically, economically, and socially, ordered Ugandan troops to seize the region of Kagera, located in northwestern Tanzania. Nyerere responded to the invasion by sending about 20,000 Tanzanian soldiers into Uganda. Although Libya had sent some troops to fight on the side of Uganda, the Tanzanian troops were joined by Ugandan rebels and exiles who had earlier escaped to Tanzania. In April 1979, Kampala, Uganda's capital, fell to Tanzanian-led forces after about six months of fighting. With Tanzania's victory, Amin fled Uganda, first to Libya and then to Saudi Arabia, where he lived until his death in August 2003. Obote's presidency was soon restored after the war between the two neighbors ended.

The Island of Zanzibar

Nicknamed the "Spice Island," Zanzibar is located in the Indian Ocean about 22 miles (35 km) away from the east coast of central Africa. Zanzibar, also known as Unguja, covers an area of about 637 square miles (1,651 square km) and measures 53 miles (85 km) from the northernmost to the southernmost tip. At 390 feet (119 m) above sea level, Masingini is the highest point on the island.

A Rich History and Heritage

Up until 1964, Zanzibar was an autonomous country. That year, Zanzibar, Pemba, and other nearby islands united with mainland Tanganyika to form the United Republic of Tanzania.

The first people to settle on Zanzibar were Africans. They were followed by Persians as early as the seventh century. Although the Persians assimilated with the locals, their legacy is still evident in twenty-first-century Zanzibar, where most people of African-Persian descent refer to themselves as "Shirazi." Shiraz is the city in present-day Iran from which the earliest Persians are believed to have emerged. Arab traders, mostly from Oman, arrived later and altered the island's sense of society.

Below: **Stone Town's Old Dispensary was built by Sir Tharia Topan, one of the wealthiest men on the island of Zanzibar. In 1990, the building was restored by the Aga Khan Trust for Culture. It is now the Stone Town Cultural Center.**

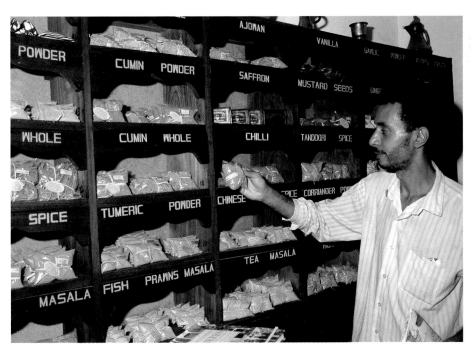

Race and class distinctions divided the population of Zanzibar, with the Arabs forming the upper class of the island. Although the Portuguese dominated the island, as well as much of East Africa, in the 1500s and 1600s, they only weakly influenced life and culture on the island. It was through the Omani Arabs that Zanzibar grew into a prosperous trade center. Cinnamon, cardamom, nutmeg, and vanilla were some of the spices that were grown on Zanzibar and other nearby islands. Cloves, however, became the region's single most important crop. In the twenty-first century, the scenic landscape and coastlines of Zanzibar attract tourist dollars in addition to supporting the traditional industries of agriculture and fishing.

Nearby Islands

Pemba Island lies to the northeast of Zanzibar and probably has more fertile land than Zanzibar. The island's Arabic name is Jazirat Al-khudrah, which means "Green Island." It is one of the world's largest producers of cloves today.

Mafia Island lies to the south of Zanzibar, close to the delta of the Rufiji River. The island has remained untouched by the modern world and the friendly people follow a traditional lifestyle. The island's Chole Bay is a protected marine area who's clear waters are perfect for snorkeling and diving.

FESTIVAL OF THE DHOW COUNTRIES

The Festival of the Dhow Countries, or the Dhow Festival, as it is commonly known, is held in Zanzibar every year. It is one of Tanzania's most important arts and cultural events. The festival attracts participants from all over the region and around the world. The event is primarily for the Dhow countries, which are defined as those that share the Indian Ocean basin. This group include the Gulf states, nations on the African continent, Iran, India, Pakistan, and islands in the Indian Ocean. The colorful festival features a variety of exhibitions, musical performances, and cultural events. The Zanzibar International Film Festival (ZIFF) is the backbone of the Dhow Festival. The year 2004 marks the seventh annual Festival of the Dhow Countries.

Kilimanjaro: The Roof of Africa

Located in northeastern Tanzania, Mount Kilimanjaro is in the administrative region of Kilimanjaro. This region forms a part of the country's border with Kenya. Moshi is the administrative capital the Kilimanjaro region.

The Sum of Three Volcanoes

Mount Kilimanjaro measures 19,340 feet (5,895 m) high and has been nicknamed the "Roof of Africa" because its summit is the highest point in Africa. A volcanic massif, Mount Kilimanjaro is composed of three main volcanoes — Mawensi, Kibo, and Shira. The massif measures about 50 miles (80 km) wide. Kibo, which is in the center and has the tallest cone, is a dormant volcano with a permanently snowcapped peak. Mawensi, which rises to about 16,893 feet (5,149 m), is the eastern and second-tallest, while Shira is the western and shortest, at 13,000 feet (3,962 m). The peaks of all three cones are often hidden from view by clouds.

AGRICULTURE IN THE KILIMANJARO REGION

Many types of cash crops are cultivated in the Kilimanjaro region. In fact, the region is the country's leading producer of barley, coffee, sugar, and wheat. Corn, beans, bananas, cotton, and potatoes are grown in smaller quantities.

Below: Erosion of its volcanic cone gives the Mawensi peak a jagged appearance. Ice occurs in patches, and the peak experiences heavy seasonal snow.

Left: Kilimanjaro is made up of three volcanoes. Kibo, the highest, is the youngest. The Chagga people live on the lower levels of the eastern and southern slopes of the mountain.

Mount Kilimanjaro National Park

Established in 1973, the Mount Kilimanjaro National Park includes not only Mount Kilimanjaro but also the forested areas around it. In 1987, UNESCO added the national park to its World Heritage List. Because different plant species thrive at different altitudes, the types of vegetation that cover the slopes of Mount Kilimanjaro mark distinct zones from base to summit. Semiarid scrub, or areas of low trees and shrubs; alpine desert; and dense forests are some of these zones. Forests that grow on the mountain's southern slopes, as well as the surrounding areas, support rich animal life. Populations of elands, duikers, elephants, buffalo, monkeys, and various birds are known to inhabit the region. Elands are large African antelopes, while duikers are a smaller type of antelope.

Scaling Mount Kilimanjaro

The Kilimanjaro peaks were first reported to the Western world in 1848. Johannes Rebmann and Johann Ludwig Krapf, both German missionaries, announced their sightings, but the news was met with disbelief because few people could believe that mountain peaks so close to the equator could be snowcapped. Forty-one years later, in 1889, German Hans Meyer and Austrian Ludwig Purtscheller made the first recorded climb to the top of Kibo. Mawensi was first scaled in 1912.

CLIMBING KIBO

Although the summit of Kibo (*below*) is Africa's highest point, people seeking to scale the volcano do not need special mountaineering equipment. Kibo's peak can be reached simply by walking. Attempting a climb in the months of April, May, and November is generally discouraged because of frequent rains during those months.

The Maasai

A Changing Culture

Traditionally, the Maasai are a seminomadic people who roamed a large area of land straddling northern Tanzania and southern Kenya. The Maasai are famous for being dedicated herdsmen, and cattle are highly valued in their culture and economy. In Tanzania, the privatization of land and the creation of national parks and protected areas in the late twentieth century greatly reduced the area of the Maasai's traditional cattle grazing land. Because many Maasai herdsmen then had insufficient pasture and water sources for their cattle, more and more Maasai have since been forced to abandon cattle herding in favor of either subsistence farming or urban living.

Up until the mid-twentieth century, centuries-old Maasai culture was relatively untouched by modern influences. Since then, concepts of property ownership and taxation have been imposed on the Maasai, who have had to adapt from a system in which resources such as grazing land and water sources were shared by all and from a trade system that was based on barter rather than the use of money.

WARRIOR TRIBE

Maasai men have a reputation for being feared warriors. This is because male members of the Maasai tribe must complete a number of initiation tasks that require great courage and skill in order to earn the title of *moran* (mor-AHN) and become recognized as men by their people. When they complete these tasks, the newly initiated men then learn the skills of warriors. As warriors, their primary duty is to protect their people from harm and their territories from loss or destruction.

Left: The daily chores of the Maasai women include fetching water, collecting firewood, cooking for the family, and milking cows. The men of the Maasai tribe, on the other hand, are expected to construct a protective fence around the homestead in which they live and care for their cattle.

Christian missionaries have converted many Maasai from their traditional beliefs. Some young Maasai have become burdened by having to learn both the skills required for their initiation rites and also modern classroom-style lessons. Although some tribal elders approve of young Maasai receiving a modern education in order to help them cope with their fast-changing world, others believe that exposing young Maasai to life in urban centers and other parts of the world turns them away from upholding and passing on the Maasai ways.

Inside the Maasai Community

The Maasai organize themselves into homesteads, each of which consists of a series of dwellings arranged in a circular fashion. Previously, several families shared one homestead, but since the implementation of property regulations, each homestead tends to be occupied by one family.

The division of labor is clear in a Maasai family. Adult men provide security to the community by serving as warriors, while uninitiated male members of the tribe contribute by herding cattle. Women, on the other hand, are expected to perform daily chores, in addition to building the family's huts, which are made from a combination of mud, sticks, grass, and cow dung.

THE MAASAI DIET

The traditional Maasai diet used the meat, milk, and blood of their cattle for food. Recently, the Maasai have grown to rely heavily on cultivated staples, such as rice, potatoes, and corn. In the past, cow's blood was viewed by the Maasai as a tonic or a health supplement. The Maasai would feed cow's blood to women who had just given birth, recently circumcised boys, the sick, and the elderly.

Opposite: Maasai men are known for their "jumping" dance. In a show of strength and agility, young warriors leap from a standing position straight into the air.

Makonde Wood Carvings

Tanzania is world famous for its wood carvings. Most of the country's wood sculptures are created by the Makonde people.

The People Behind the Art Form

The Makonde are a Bantu-speaking people who live in the region that straddles southeastern Tanzania and northeastern Mozambique. The Ruvuma River separates the different Makonde groups. They are mainly an agricultural people who still practice the slash-and-burn method of farming. The Makonde have been able to retain many of their original ethnic traditions because their isolated location has allowed them to remain relatively untouched by foreign influences.

MWENGE MARKET

Many Makonde carvers sell their works at the Mwenge market, located in Dar es Salaam. Buyers of Makonde carvings can purchase a completed carving, a partially completed carving that will be finished for them, or a piece of raw wood that will be carved to order.

Left: The Makonde trace their lineage through the female side of the family. It is not uncommon for them to carve statues of the female form. These sculptures are used for ancestor worship.

Left: Makonde carvers incorporate the natural irregularities of mpingo trunks into their designs. Because the wood is hard and difficult to shape, larger carvings can take up to a year to finish.

The Art of the People

To create their exquisite works, the Makonde work with the ebony known as African blackwood (*Dalbergia Melanoxylon*) or *mpingo* (m-PEE-ngoh). The heart of the mpingo tree is dense and has a deep brown or black color, while the bark of the tree is lighter in color and softer. This combination makes the wood ideal for carving. The Makonde are known for their *mapiko* (mah-PEE-koh) masks, which are required during rituals that initiate boys into manhood. A matrilineal society, the Makonde carve female statues that are used for ancestor worship.

Traditionally, Makonde carvings have nature as a theme. In recent years, three contemporary styles of carving have emerged. The most popular is *Shetani* (sheh-TA-nih), which is Swahili for "little devil" and involves carvings of demonlike creatures. The style known as ujamaa is based on the spirit of the family or the village. Ujamaa carvings are usually created out of a single piece of wood and have a large central figure at the top watching over people engaged in everyday activities. The third style is the most abstract, encouraging the carver to work with forms. It is known as *mawingu* (ma-WHIN-goo) which is Swahili for "clouds."

Nyerere: The Father of a Nation

An Educator, a Leader, and a Visionary

Julius Kambarage Nyerere (1922–1999) was born in a small village near the country's northern city of Musoma and Lake Victoria. At Makerere College, in Uganda, he trained as a teacher. When he graduated, he returned to Tanganyika and taught for some years. In 1949, Nyerere received a government scholarship to pursue a master's degree in history and political economy at the University of Edinburgh in Scotland. Nyerere's interest in his country's politics took shape in the 1950s. By 1960, the Tanganyika African National Union (TANU), a political party he helped found in 1954 and then led as president, won the parliamentary elections in a landslide victory. Nyerere served as Tanzania's president from 1964 to 1985.

During his presidency, Nyerere began policies and programs aimed at creating equal opportunities and progress for his people through lifelong education. Under his leadership, Tanzania was a firm and active supporter of freedom and peace throughout the African continent. Although the success of his ideas was short-lived, Nyerere's foresight and compassion endeared him to many people both within and outside of Tanzania.

Left: **Julius Nyerere once said that "The development of a country is brought about by people, not by money. Money, and the wealth it represents, is the result and not the basis of development."**

Left: Julius Nyerere was a strong supporter of the liberation of African nations. Not surprisingly, he became the first chairman of the Frontline States, a group which was fighting to establish majority rule in Zimbabwe, South Africa, and Namibia. The Frontline States consisted of Tanzania, Angola, Mozambique, Botswana, and Zambia.

His Vision

Nyerere's way of encouraging reform and progress for his nation was based on principles of equality, education, and self-reliance. Nyerere laid out his policies in the Arusha Declaration of 1967. Some historians have called Nyerere's movement "Tanzanian socialism," with the most prominent example of this being the ujamaa system. Ujamaa is a Swahili word that means "familyhood." In Nyerere's Tanzania, ujamaa was a system of organized villages in which Tanzanian subsistence farmers came together to live and work on communal farmlands that the government supported with as much infrastructure and services as it could afford. The purpose of this system was to improve agricultural productivity and the living standards of rural Tanzanians through the pooling of labor and resources.

Nyerere believed that the stability of his country depended on the people's unity. As a result, he developed policies that encouraged Tanzanians to recognize themselves and one another as belonging to one nation, rather than their indigenous groups. To bring together more than 120 ethnic groups, Nyerere made Swahili the country's official language. This allowed Tanzanians, regardless of ethnicity or religion, to communicate and develop shared interests and concerns. Nyerere also worked to eliminate corruption in his government and provide free education and health care to all Tanzanians.

WITH UTMOST RESPECT

The work of Nyerere has undeniably shaped modern Tanzania and will, in some ways, continue to shape its future. The deep love and respect that ordinary Tanzanians have for Nyerere is reflected in the way they refer to him. To many Tanzanians, Nyerere is *known as mwalimu* (mwah-LIH-moo), which means "teacher." Tanzanian coins call him *Baba wa Taifa* (BAH-bah wah tah-IH-fah), which means "Father of the Nation."

Paying a Bride Price

What is a Bride Price?

In Tanzania, as is the case in much of East Africa, a bride price is paid by a man or his family to the family of the woman he seeks to marry in order to win approval for the marriage. A bride price can consist of a sum of money, a collection of gifts, or a combination of the two. Marriage gifts that may be given as part of a bride price include food, cloth, cows, and goats. Some cultures in other parts of the world have a similar practice called paying a dowry. In some of these other cultures, however, a dowry is presented by a woman's family to her future husband or his family.

A Controversial Custom

Many traditional East Africans, including Tanzanians, believe that any marriage, whether religious or civil, is not official or complete if the bride price has not been paid. In the Maasai culture, marriages are prearranged and bride prices are paid when the girl is born. If the female refuses to marry her intended husband, the bride price has to be returned. In addition, the groom may charge interest to the girl's family.

Below: **For the Sukuma and Maasai peoples, the bride price is normally paid in cattle or livestock. Other indigenous peoples who still practice the tradition of paying bride prices include the Makonde, Nyakyusa, Nyamwezi and Nyika.**

Although some women feel honored or valued if their future husbands paid high bride prices to their families, an increasing number of women are also suffering precisely because they fetched high bride prices. Critics of the bride-price custom say that the practice allows a woman to be abused by her husband. A husband may believe that he has rightfully purchased his wife, and he may, therefore, feel that he can do whatever he likes to her because she is his property. Defenders of the bride price, on the other hand, point out that the custom began as a meaningful and sincere gesture of thanks from the groom or his family to the bride's family for having brought her up well.

Marriage traditionally carries a great deal of meaning for Tanzanian women. Upon marrying, Tanzanian women gain not only the right to own land and property, but also access to labor and other resources that exist in their communities at the time. When wives become mothers, their importance in the household increases.

Above: At a Maasai wedding ceremony, it is possible to see some guests dressed in traditional Maasai costumes and others with modern Western clothes. Maasai culture allows a man to have more than one wife, as long as he able to pay the bride prices. Males who own more cattle are more likely to have multiple wives.

Tingatinga Art

The Founder

Born in 1932, Edward Saidi Tingatinga was a member of the Makua people. The son of subsistence farmers, Tingatinga moved to Dar es Salaam in an effort to earn a living in the city. He moved from one employer to another. One day, while he was in between jobs, he began painting on square chipboards using house paint. Tingatinga painted what he knew: scenes of everyday life, which included animals, birds, the cultural beliefs of Tanzanians, and images of village life.

People liked his paintings and were willing to pay money for them. It soon became obvious to Tingatinga that he could earn a living from his paintings. He influenced his family and friends, and before long, he and a small group were producing this art form and developing it further.

Tingatinga's art soon caught the attention of the National Development Cooperation, which bought a number of his paintings and organized an exhibition of the works. This raised the profile of the art form and soon made it widely known.

A NEW BUILDING

Helvetas is a Swiss association that works to promote culture and education in rural areas. During 1996 and 1997, Helvetas arranged for an exhibition of Tingatinga paintings to be shown in various towns around Switzerland. Art pieces were sold and the money that was collected went towards the construction of a new building for the Tingatinga Arts Cooperative Society in Dar es Salaam. The new building is being used by the members of the Society as a workshop for classes, a storehouse, a gallery, and a showroom for sales.

Left: Wild animals are a common motif in Tingatinga art. They are drawn using bright and vivid colors.

In 1972, Tingatinga met an untimely death when he was mistaken for a robber by the police and shot. He was only forty years old, and his body of work was fairly small. His death, however, was not the end of his art form, as his followers continue to produce what has become known as Tingatinga art.

The Art

The first thing that one notices about Tingatinga art is its bright and vibrant colors. The paintings may be stylized, but they vividly capture subjects that are easy to identify. The themes have remained true to Edward Tingatinga's original pieces. Today, Tingatinga artwork portrays scenes of wildlife, village life, rituals, and even magic and sorcery. What has changed is the way the paintings are presented. Tingatinga artists of today draw inspiration not just from what is around them but also from each other. They share ideas and hone their skills, and the results are finished products that are very polished. This has earned the style a reputation as pop art that has a sensitive and harmonious feel.

A directive from the government caused the forming of the Tingatinga Arts Cooperative Society. Its purpose is to teach the art form and make it better known around the world.

The Wonders of the Serengeti

The Serengeti region is composed of the Serengeti National Park, the Ngorongoro Conservation Area, and a number of smaller reserves in northern Tanzania, as well as the Maasai Mara Game Reserve in southwestern Kenya.

Serengeti National Park

Declared a World Heritage site by UNESCO in 1981, the Serengeti National Park covers a vast area of nearly 5,700 square miles (14,763 square km). *Serengeti* means "endless plain" in the Maasai tongue, and the park's mainly savanna landscape includes grasslands, woodlands, marshes, riverside forests, and evergreen forests. Plant life in the park can be unusual, with species such as the sausage tree (*Kigelia africana*), the strangle fig (*Ficus thonningii*), the yellow fever tree (*Acacia xanthophloea*), and the toothbrush tree (*Salvadora persica*).

Animal life in the park is intensely rich, including not only the famous African "big five" — lions, leopards, elephants, buffaloes, and rhinoceroses — but also numerous species of primates, wild dogs, wild cats, mongooses, reptiles, and nearly five hundred species of birds. Hippopotamuses, giraffes,

CONTROLLED AREAS IN THE SERENGETI

Surrounding the Serengeti National Park and the Ngorongoro Conservation Area are several other protected areas. Joining the Serengeti National Park and the Ngorongoro Conservation Area, the Loliondo Controlled Area lies to the east of the national park and to the north of the conservation area. The Grumeti and Ikorongo Controlled Areas are located along the northwestern fringes of the national park. The Maswa Game Reserve extends from the park's southwestern border, and the Maasai Mara Game Reserve in Kenya borders the part to the north.

Left: In the Serengeti, herds of zebras make an annual trek from one watering hole to another. The gnu and gazelles of the Serengeti also migrate in search of water.

antelopes, and ostriches are just some of the larger and more prominent safari animals, while spitting cobras, cheetahs, and crocodiles are some of the feared species.

Every year, about two hundred thousand zebras and more than one million gnu cause a spectacle and a din in the national park when they migrate in search of water and new pasture. In loud, stampeding herds, the animals first travel south from the northern hills late in the year and then turn westward between May and June of the following year.

Above: **The Serengeti region only became known to the Western world in 1913, when American Stewart Edward White saw it while leading an expedition from Nairobi. The Serengeti was part of the inspiration for the Hollywood animated film *The Lion King* (1994).**

Ngorongoro Conservation Area

The Ngorongoro Crater is the world's largest unbroken caldera — covering nearly 100 square miles (260 square km) and measuring about 2,000 feet (610 m) deep. The diverse animal population and types of vegetation that thrive there have led some people to describe the caldera as a miniature of East Africa. Hyenas, cape buffaloes, rhinoceroses, hippopotamuses, and zebras are some of the animals that roam the crater floor. The crater is also the only source of freshwater and mineral salts for 50 miles (80 km). Established in 1959, the Ngorongoro Conservation Area was declared a World Heritage site by UNESCO in 1979. The Olduvai Gorge, an archaeological site that contains fossils of early humans, is situated within the Ngorongoro Conservation Area.

Zanzibar's House of Wonders

Located in Stone Town on the island of Zanzibar, the House of Wonders was once the ceremonial palace of the Omani sultans. Also known as Beit al-Ajaib, this impressive seafront building was, and still is today, one of the largest buildings on the island.

The History of the House

In 1883, the House of Wonders was built by Seyyid Barghash, who ruled from 1870 to 1888 as the third sultan of Zanzibar, on the former site of a queen's residence. The house was one of the six palaces that Barghash erected and was used mainly as an official reception hall. In 1896, Seyyid Khalid, a son of Barghash, attempted to claim the throne after the death his father's successor. At the time, Zanzibar was a British protectorate, and the British did not support Khalid's claim to the throne. During what is now called the shortest war in

Above: **The House of Wonders (right) and another sultan's palace stand along Zanzibar's waterfront.**

history, the House of Wonders sustained some damage when the British bombarded Stone Town. The lighthouse was destroyed, but it was later replaced by a large clock tower.

After the war, the House of Wonders was the place of residence for two successive sultans. In 1911, it was converted into government offices. Today, the building serves as the Museum of Zanzibar History and Swahili Civilization.

The Wonders of the House

When it was built, the House of Wonders was the tallest and one of the largest buildings in the country. Designed by a British marine engineer, the House of Wonders was the first building in Zanzibar that had electricity, running water, and an elevator. The building's architecture was extraordinary for its time. Its cast iron columns allowed a wide balcony made of reinforced concrete to run along all four of its sides. The columns also allowed the House of Wonders to have very high ceilings, making the building even more imposing. The open galleries that surround the covered courtyard could be reached only by a majestic marble stairway. Some of the doors on the inside of the house bear exquisite carvings of passages from the Qur'an.

Opposite: **The House of Wonders was damaged when the British bombarded Zanzibar in 1896. The lighthouse, which stood above the main building, was completely destroyed. It was later replaced with a clock tower that still exists today.**

74

RELATIONS WITH NORTH AMERICA

Tanzania is one of the more stable countries on the African continent. The country enjoys good relations not just with many of its African neighbors but also with the United States and Canada. In an effort to help the country raise the quality of life of Tanzania's citizens, the United States has generously made funds, expert personnel, and other assistance available. USAID, an independent government agency, allocates a yearly budget to help Tanzania achieve their goals. The U.S. Peace Corps is a constant presence in Tanzania, and its close relationship with Tanzanians mirrors the relationship between the two countries.

Opposite: **Many U.S. products, such as Coca-Cola, can be found in parts of Tanzania.**

Tanzania has also found a faithful ally in Canada, a country that has provided monetary aid and the hand of friendship. Both countries are constantly cooperating with the United Nations and the British Commonwealth to eradicate racial discrimination and any form of hegemony.

The United States, Canada, and Tanzania participate together in cultural and educational exchanges, such as the Fulbright program. Under the Fulbright program, professionals and students from the United States, Tanzania, and other countries get an opportunity to study, teach, or do research in a foreign country.

Above: **In 2000, when President Bill Clinton of the United States arrived in Arusha, he hoped to witness the start of an era of peace in Burundi. This was not to be. Nonetheless, Clinton and Tanzanian president Benjamin Mkapa forged new alliances of their own.**

Relations with the United States

In the past, relations between the United States and Tanzania have generally been amicable. For a while, the United States had two embassies in Tanzania, one on the mainland and one on the island of Zanzibar. In 1979, however, the Zanzibari consulate was closed. After August 7, 1998, relations strengthened when the U.S. embassy in Dar es Salaam was bombed by terrorists, killing twelve people and injuring eighty-five. In the wake of the world's outrage, the United States and Tanzania formed closer ties, especially in the areas of internal security and antiterrorist activities.

In September 1999, President Benjamin Mkapa visited the United States with a group of representatives from his country's business community. Mkapa's aim was to show the United States that Tanzania was serious about increasing the level of trade and investment between the two countries. He even went so far as to change some of Tanzania's laws so that economic cooperation would be made easier. Impressed with Mkapa's leadership and commitment to enhancing the quality of life for Tanzanians, the United States has continued to provide assistance to Tanzania. U.S. authorities hope that Tanzania will be able to improve its environment and health care, strengthen its democratic process, and build up businesses in the private sector.

Below: **Tanzanian president Julius Nyerere visited U.S. president John F. Kennedy in 1961, just after both began their respective terms in office.**

Relations with Canada

Tanzanian president Benjamin Mkapa served as the Tanzanian High Commissioner to Canada from 1982 to 1983, but ties between Canada and Tanzania go back to the time of Tanganyika's independence in 1961. The two countries are part of the Commonwealth, each having been a British colony in the past. Since 1961, Canada has contributed more then CAN $1 billion in aid to assist Tanzania in many areas, including health, education, agriculture, and railways. Many Canadian companies have also invested money in Tanzania's mining and power industries.

Tanzania is one of the countries in the Heavily Indebted Poor Country (HIPC) Initiative, a program that aims to reduce the debt amount a country owes to a sustainable level. Under the Canadian Debt Moratorium, HIPC countries that owe money to Canada will have their debt written off once the country meets the conditions set down by the initiative. In November 2001, Tanzania achieved the conditions set down by HIPC. As a result, Canada canceled Tanzania's outstanding debt. Canada also supports Tanzania's efforts in the Poverty Reduction Strategy, a program that aims to reduce poverty in the country.

Above: **A village hotel in the city of Iramba, located in the Mara region. U.S. presence, as seen by the Pepsi Cola sign, is evident even in small villages.**

USAID in Tanzania

The United States has a history assisting other countries. Through the U.S. Agency for International Development (USAID), an agency linked to the U.S. government, the United States helps improve the lives of many people living in developing countries.

To the United States, Tanzania is a positive force in Africa. Believing that Tanzania can play a role in resolving conflicts among other African nations, the United States offers help so that the country will better develop economically and politically. Every year, Tanzania receives about U.S. $20 million in aid.

USAID has a number of programs operating in Tanzania. The agency has recently made contributions in several areas. The first was in the area of family and health. An immunization program was put into place and vitamin A supplements were given to five million children. In an effort to reduce the number of AIDS cases in the country, a campaign to educate, test, and counsel people was introduced. Funds were also used to develop the leadership team of the Tanzania Commission for AIDS (TACAIDS) and the Reproductive and Child Health Section (RCHS).

Above: **Tanzania's infant mortality rate is high. USAID hopes to improve living conditions in rural areas. One of Tanzania's USAID programs works to immunize children against diseases.**

FOREIGN ASSISTANCE AGENCY

In 1961, the passing of the Foreign Assistance Act created the U.S. Agency for International Development (USAID). The agency's fundamental aims are to help improve the standard of living for citizens in developing countries, promote democracy, and encourage economic growth.

USAID also supports cooperation between the public and private sectors, especially in the areas of HIV/AIDS issues and the management of natural resources. In 2003, with help from USAID, the Tanzania Parliamentary AIDS Coalition (TAPAC) was able to lay the groundwork for decreasing the local and national and impact of HIV/AIDS. USAID also assisted a local nongovernmental organization (NGO) and the government in drafting a new law to protect the environment.

The third area to which USAID contributes in Tanzania is the conservation of the country's coastal regions. USAID was also able to promote the economic gains and investment potential of Tanzania's coastal regions.

USAID has helped small enterprises, especially those in the agricultural industry, gain a foothold in business. Under some USAID programs, farmers were able to get better prices for their products, and the building of roads in rural areas helped to provide access to potential markets.

USAID has also given assistance to the children of the victims of the terrorist bombing of the U.S. embassy in Dar es Salaam. In 2002, sixteen children, all offspring of the bombing victims, were provided with educational aid by USAID.

Left: **Tanzania's coastal regions are home to a flourishing fishing and shrimp catching industry. Because of this, the coasts are a potential source of income and can greatly enhance the country's economy, especially if they attract foreign investment. It is, therefore, crucial that effort be made to conserve the coasts.**

Other U.S. Financial Aid

In June 2002, a train crash near Dodoma killed more than 280 people. This incident was the worst train disaster in Tanzanian history. The United States provided emergency assistance in the form of U.S. $50,000. These funds were used to purchase medical supplies to help treat and care for the victims of the crash.

The Ambassador's Fund for Cultural Preservation is used to help preserve the cultural heritage of less developed countries. Its resources can be used to benefit a historical site, manuscript, language, traditional music and dance style, or collection. In September 2002, the United States donated more than U.S. $25,000 from this fund to the Dhow Countries Music Academy. The money was directed toward the purchase of musical instruments and the salaries of teachers who could teach and spread taarab, a traditional form of music in Tanzania.

The United States is the largest contributor to the Global Fund to Fight AIDS, Tuberculosis, and Malaria. In February 2003, the Fund announced that more than U.S. $2.3 million

Left: One main area of focus for the Peace Corps in Tanzania is education. Volunteers are often assigned to the country's schools as teachers.

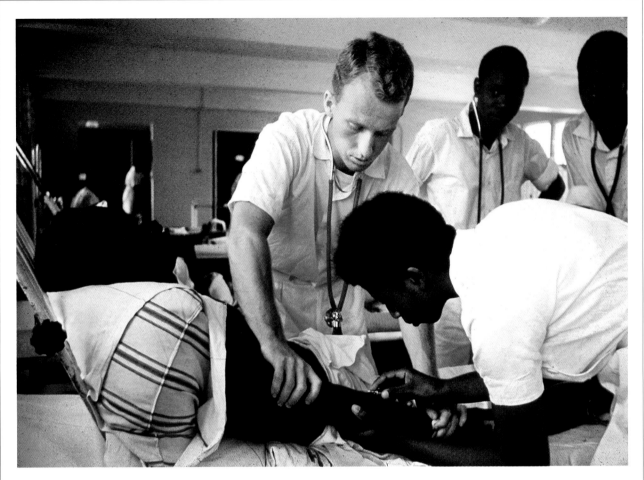

had been designated to fight HIV/AIDS in Zanzibar, where the number of HIV/AIDS cases has increased sharply since the 1980s.

Above: **AIDS is a major problem in Tanzania. In some hospitals, half the total patients admitted suffer from this disease. Peace Corps volunteers who work in the hospitals face the challenge of educating Tanzanians about HIV/AIDS and raising their awareness of how serious the disease is.**

The Peace Corps in Tanzania

In 1962, Peace Corps volunteers first arrived in Tanzania. The work of these volunteers continued until 1969 when the Corps withdrew from the country because of political differences. The period of separation lasted about ten years. In 1979, the Peace Corps returned to Tanzania once again. In 1983, the Corps celebrated ten years of service in the country.

When the Gulf War started in 1990, volunteers were asked to return home for security reasons. By 1992, the Peace Corps was again firmly entrenched on Tanzanian soil. The year 2002 marks the thirtieth year of Peace Corps service in Tanzania. Currently, there are eighty-two Peace Corps volunteers in the country. They work in three main areas: environment, school health, and education.

Left: **It took two years for the various political leaders of Burundi to reach some semblance of a peace agreement. In 2000, the peace negotiations in Arusha were plagued with problems. One reason for the breakdown in these talks was the absence of the two main rebel groups. Eventually, the leaders present at the talks signed an outline of a peace agreement.**

A United States President in Tanzania

President Bill Clinton made two visits to Africa while he was in office. The first was in 1998, during which he toured Botswana, Ghana, Rwanda, Senegal, South Africa, and Uganda. His second visit was in 2000, when he spent four days in Nigeria, Tanzania, and Egypt. Clinton's visit to Tanzania was timed to coincide with the possible signing of a peace treaty between the warring factions of Burundi. Unfortunately, hours before his arrival, the various parties were still unhappy with the terms of a deal negotiated by Nelson Mandela, and an agreement could not be reached. Mandela, the former South African president, had been acting as the peace negotiator for two years and had hoped that Clinton's presence would help bring about a peaceful solution to the problems. Clinton urged the Burundians to settle their disputes. Finally, the political leaders of Burundi who were present at the talks agreed to sign a framework for a treaty whose key points would be negotiated at a later date.

In the short time that he was in the Tanzanian city of Arusha, Clinton met with President Benjamin Mkapa to discuss Tanzania's debt-ridden economy and possible solutions to the economic problems that hinder the country's development. Both presidents also signed an agreement relating to air transport connections between the two countries.

Visitors to Tanzania

In July 2003, a delegation consisting of students, teachers, and professionals from Chicago visited Tanzania's Arusha Secondary School in order to set up a computer lab. The trip was called the "Peace Journey." The group spent three weeks in the region of Arusha, where they, together with the teachers and students of the school, laid the groundwork for the computer lab, helped to conduct Internet classes, and spoke with community leaders.

In September 2003, six teachers from the Seattle public school district visited Tanzania for two weeks as part of an exchange program between the two countries for education professionals. While in Tanzania, the teachers from the United States lived with their Tanzanian counterparts in order to immerse themselves in another culture. The Seattle teachers also trained a group of Tanzanian teachers in computer studies. During their trip, the American teachers found that teachers in Tanzania had trouble being creative in the classroom because of scarce resources and the rigid curriculum required in Tanzania.

Left: **President Bill Clinton made two state visits to the African continent. It was on his second trip in 2000 that he stopped in Tanzania for eight hours. Clinton's meeting with President Benjamin Mkapa of Tanzania was eventful. Clinton praised the East African nation, in particular for reacting quickly and efficiently to the bombing of the U.S. embassy in Dar es Salaam in 1998.**

Tanzanians in North America

Few people know that Freddie Mercury, lead vocalist of the pop group Queen, was born on the island of Zanzibar. Born Farrokh Bulsara in 1946, Mercury moved with his family to India in 1947. In 1963, the family moved again, this time to the United Kingdom. In 1971, Mercury teamed up with Brian May, John Deacon, and Roger Taylor to form Queen. In 1975, the group achieved its first U.S. success with "Killer Queen," which would be the first of many Queen songs to top the music charts, not just in the United States but also around the world. Two of Queen's songs — "We Are the Champions" and "We Will Rock You" — became so popular that they are now used as rousing chants in sports arenas in the United States and the United Kingdom.

In the early 1980s, Queen's success suffered a slight setback, but the group's popularity revived after a spectacular performance at Live Aid in 1985. Sadly,

Opposite: **Freddie Mercury was the only son of Bomi and Jer Bulsara. Mercury was part of a number of bands before he became a member of Queen in 1971.**

Freddie Mercury passed away from AIDS in 1991. Four years later, the remaining members of Queen announced the disbanding of the group. In 2001, Queen was inducted into the Rock and Roll Hall of Fame.

Above: **U.S. State Secretary Dean Rusk (*left*), Tanzanian president Julius Nyerere (*center*), and U.S. president John F. Kennedy (*right*) observe a solemn moment as they listen to the national anthems of their two countries.**

Tanzanian Visitors to the United States

When John F. Kennedy (1917–1963) was president of the United States from 1961 to 1963, President Julius Nyerere paid him a visit at the White House. Nyerere was the second visitor to the Oval Office while Kennedy was in office. Nyerere was said to have great admiration for Kennedy.

Over the years, the number of Tanzanians studying in the United States have increased. In 2001, there were 1,528 Tanzanian students in the United States. In 2002, this figure jumped to 1,824, an 18.7 percent increase. Since 1998, the total number of Tanzanian students in the United States has doubled. This is because many Tanzanian teenagers are interested in continuing their tertiary education at colleges and universities in the United States.

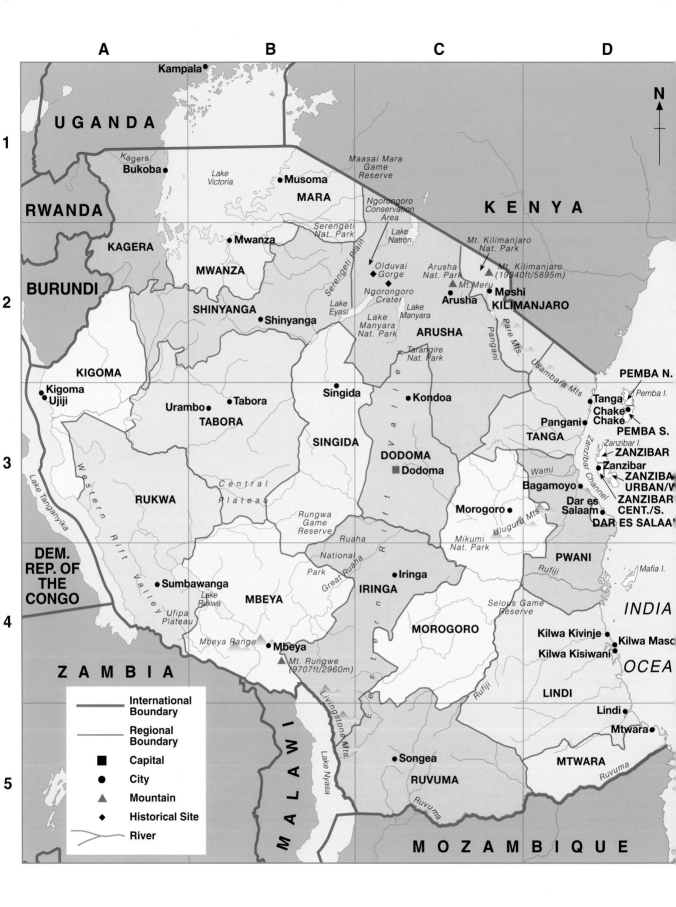

A

B

C

D

N

Kampala ●

U G A N D A

1

Kagera

Bukoba ●

RWANDA

MARA

Musoma ●

Lake Victoria

Maasai Mara Game Reserve

K E N Y A

KAGERA

Ngorongoro Conservation Area

Lake Natron

Mt. Kilimanjaro Nat. Park

BURUNDI

Mwanza ●

MWANZA

Serengeti Nat. Park

▲ *Mt.Meru*

Arusha Nat. Park

▲ Mt. Kilimanjaro (19340ft/5895m)

Moshi ●

2

SHINYANGA

Serengeti Plain

◆ *Olduvai Gorge*

Arusha ●

KILIMANJARO

Shinyanga ●

Lake Eyasi

Ngorongoro Crater

Lake Manyara

Lake Manyara Nat. Park

ARUSHA

Pangani

Pare Mts.

Usambara Mts

PEMBA N.

KIGOMA

Tarangire Nat. Park

Tanga ●

Pemba I.

Kigoma ●

Ujiji ●

Urambo ●

Tabora ●

Singida ●

Kondoa ●

Chake Chake ●

PEMBA S.

TABORA

Pangani ●

Zanzibar I.

TANGA

3

Lake Tanganyika

Western Rift Valley

SINGIDA

DODOMA

■ **Dodoma**

Central Plateau

Wami

Zanzibar Channel

Zanzibar ●

ZANZIBAR

RUKWA

Rungwa Game Reserve

Morogoro ●

Uluguru Mts.

Bagamoyo ●

Dar es Salaam ●

ZANZIBAR URBAN/V

ZANZIBAR CENT./S.

DAR ES SALAA

DEM. REP. OF THE CONGO

Ruaha

National

Park

Great Ruaha

Mikumi Nat. Park

PWANI

Rufiji

Mafia I.

INDIA

Sumbawanga ●

Iringa ●

IRINGA

Selous Game Reserve

Kilwa Kivinje ●

4

MBEYA

Lake Rukwa

Ufipa Plateau

MOROGORO

Kilwa Masc ●

Kilwa Kisiwani ●

OCEA

Mbeya Range

▲ **Mbeya** ●

▲ Mt. Rungwe (9707ft/2960m)

Eastern Rift Valley

Rufiji

LINDI

Lindi ●

Z A M B I A

Livingstone Mts.

Mtwara ●

M A L A W I

Lake Nyasa

Songea ●

RUVUMA

MTWARA

Ruvuma

5

	International Boundary
	Regional Boundary
■	Capital
●	City
▲	Mountain
◆	Historical Site
～	River

M O Z A M B I Q U E

Above: The Serengeti National Park is home to a wide variety of wildlife species, including the majestic cheetah.

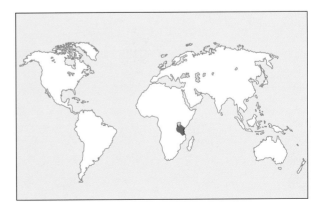

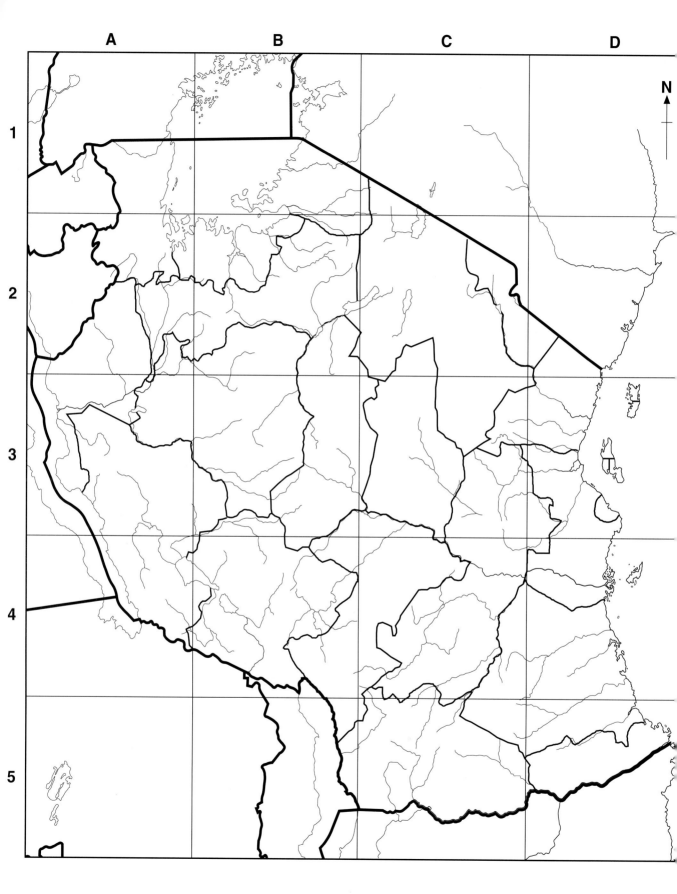

How Is Your Geography?

Learning to identify the main geographical areas and points of a country can be challenging. Although it may seem difficult at first to memorize the locations and spellings of major cities or the names of mountain ranges, rivers, deserts, lakes, and other prominent physical features, the end result of this effort can be very rewarding. Places you previously did not know existed will suddenly come to life when referred to in world news, whether in newspapers, television reports, other books and reference sources, or on the Internet. This knowledge will make you feel a bit closer to the rest of the world, with its fascinating variety of cultures and physical geography.

This map can be duplicated for use in a classroom. (PLEASE DO NOT WRITE IN THIS BOOK!) Students can then fill in any requested information on their individual map copies. The student can also make a copy of the map and use it as a study tool to practice identifying place names and geographical features on his or her own.

Below: **The Maasai are known for their brightly colored and intricately patterned beaded collars.**

Tanzania at a Glance

Official Name   United Republic of Tanzania

Capital   Dodoma

Offical Languages English, Swahili

Population   35,922,454

Land Area   342,100 square miles (886,037 sq km)

Regions   Arusha, Dar es Salaam, Dodoma, Iringa, Kagera, Kigoma, Kilimanjaro, Lindi, Mara, Mbeya, Morogoro, Mtwara, Mwanza, Pemba North, Pemba South, Pwani, Rukwa, Ruvuma, Shinyanga, Singida, Tabora, Tanga, Zanzibar Central/South, Zanzibar North, Zanzibar Urban/West

Highest Point   Mount Kilimanjaro 19,340 feet (5,895 m)

Border Countries   Burundi, Democratic Republic of the Congo (DRC), Kenya, Malawi, Mozambique, Rwanda, Uganda, Zambia

Natural Resources Coal, diamonds, gemstones, gold, hydropower, iron ore, natural gas, nickel, phosphates, tin

Main Religions   Christianity, indigenous beliefs, Islam

Literacy   78.2 percent

Important Festivals Christmas, Easter, Farmers' Day, Idd-El-Fitr, Idd-El-Hajj, International Trade Fair, Independence Day, Mwalimu Nyerere Day, Union Day, Zanzibar Revolution Day

Major Industries   Agricultural processing (sisal twine and sugar), cement, diamond and gold mining, fertilizer, oil refining, salt, shoes, textiles, wood products

Main Exports   Cashew nuts, coffee, cotton, gold

Main Imports   Consumer goods, crude oil, industrial raw materials, machinery, transportation equipment

Currency   Tanzanian Shilling (1,131 TZS = U.S. $1 in 2004)

Opposite: **Bao is a board game that is popular among Tanzanians.**

Glossary

Tanzanian Vocabulary

Baba wa Taifa (BAH-bah wah tah-IH-fah): Father of the Nation.

bao (BA-ow): a board game.

Bunge (BUN-gay): the National Assembly.

chakacha (cha-KA-cha): an indigenous dance similar to belly dancing.

dhow (DA-ow): a type of ship used by early Arab traders that has at least two masts supporting large, triangular sails.

lelemama (LEH-leh-MA-ma): a dance with complex hand movements.

maandazi (man-DA-see): a fried sweet bread.

mapiko (man-PEE-koh): ritual masks of the Makonde.

marimba (ma-RIM-ba): a finger piano that consists of a range of metal springs of varying lengths that resonate against a wooden box.

mawingu (ma-WIHN-goo): Makonde wood carvings that use abstract forms.

mishikaki (mih-shih-KA-kih): meat broiled over a charcoal fire.

moran (mor-AHN): an initiated Maasai man.

mpingo (m-PEE-ngoh): African blackwood.

mtindo (mu-EEN-doh): a form of dance music.

mwalimu (mwah-LIH-moo): teacher.

ngoma (ng-OH-ma): a traditional style of dance and music.

ruga-ruga (ROO-ga ROO-ga): Ngoni mercenaries from southern Africa.

shetani (sheh-TA-nih): a style of Makonde wood carving that features demonlike creatures.

taarab (taa-RAB): a traditional form of music in which poetry is sung.

ugali (u-GA-lih): a dough-like porridge made from cassava, cornmeal, millet, or sorghum.

uhuru (oo-HU-roo): freedom.

ujamaa (OO-ja-MAa): Swahili for "familyhood;" the name for a form of economic cooperation and tribal harmony introduced by Julius Nyerere; also a style of wood carving that illustrates people in everyday activities.

English Vocabulary

advocated: supported; upheld as correct.

allure: attraction, charm, or appeal.

assets: items of value.

assimilated: adopted the practices, customs, and attitudes of the dominant cultural group.

autonomous: self-governing.

bombarded: repeatedly bombed.

caldera: a large, basinlike depression resulting from the explosion or collapse of the center of a volcano.

chapatis: round, flat breads that are usually made of whole wheat flour and cooked on a griddle.

communicable diseases: diseases that can be easily transmitted.

crop rotation: the system of growing different types of crops on the same plot of land, one year after another, in order to make the best use of the soil.

curriculum: the course of study offered by a school.

dispensaries: places where medical or dental aid is given.

dormant: inactive; as if sleeping.

durable: long-lasting.

embellished: made beautiful by adding ornamentation.

exile: the state in which a person is forced to stay away from his or her country.

exotic: exciting and unusual.

harem: a sultan's wives and concubines.

hegemony: one group of people being dominant over other groups.

hominid: a mammal that belongs to the group that includes modern humans and their extinct ancestors.

implemented: put into practice.

inoculate: to inject an organic substance into the body to prevent or to treat a particular disease.

intrigued: aroused the curiosity.

legacy: anything handed down from an ancestor.

mandate: a formal order from a person or organization with higher authority.

mandatory: compulsory; something which must be done.

massif: a mass of rock that is a part of Earth's crust that has been pushed upward by immense moving forces originating beneath the crust.

matrilineal: tracing a person's heritage through the mother's side of the family.

melancholy: a depressed state of mind.

monogamy: the practice of being married to only one person at a time.

nurture: to develop.

pidgin: the simplified form of a language used for communication between people who speak different languages.

plantains: a type of banana that needs to be cooked before it can be eaten.

poachers: people who illegally enter protected areas or private property to hunt animals or catch fish.

principality: a territory that is traditionally governed by a prince.

renowned: celebrated; well-known.

resonator: a device that enriches a musical tone by vibrating along with it.

samosas: small, deep-fried triangular pastries filled with spicy meat or vegetables.

slash-and-burn method: a type of farming where forest areas are cleared in order to create plots of land for growing crops.

standard: the personal flag of a member of a royal family.

stature: the natural height of a person in an upright position.

subsistence farming: farming that produces enough food only for the farmer and his family.

successive: one following another, without any interruption.

thrive: to flourish; prosper.

undulating: moving in such a way that gives an appearance of a wave moving.

unicameral: consisting of only one legislative body.

unscrupulous: unethical; having no regard for morals or principles.

vibrant: striking; giving a sense of life.

vocational: related to a trade that can be used to earn a living.

More Books to Read

Climbing Mount Kilimanjaro. Stephen Carmichael (Medi-Ed Press)

My Life With the Chimpanzees. Jane Goodall (Simon & Schuster)

Serengeti Migration: Africa's Animals On the Move. Lisa Lindblad (Hyperion Press)

Serengeti Plain. *Wonders of the World* series. Terri Willis (Raintree/Steck Vaughn)

Sukuma. *Heritage Library of African Peoples* series. Aimee Bessire and Mark H.C. Bessire (Rosen Publishing Group)

Tanzania. *Cultures of the World* series. Jay Heale (Benchmark Books)

Tanzania in Pictures. *Visual Geography* series. Marylee S. Crofts (Lerner Publications Company)

Videos

Africa — The Serengeti. (E-Realbiz.Com)

East Africa, Tanzania and Zanzibar. (Lonely Planet)

Kilimanjaro: To the Roof of Africa. (Ventura Distribution)

National Geographic's Tanzania —Thorn Tree Country. (Questar, Inc.)

National Geographic's Wings Over the Serengeti. (National Geographic)

Web Sites

usembassy.state.gov/tanzania/

www.cia.gov/cia/publications/factbook/geos/tz.html

www.sas.upenn.edu/African_Studies/NEH/thome.htm

www.serengeti.org

www.tanzania.go.tz/index2E.html

www.usaid.gov/tz/

Due to the dynamic nature of the Internet, some web sites stay current longer than others. To find additional web sites, use a reliable search engine with one or more of the following keywords to help you locate information about Tanzania. Keywords: *Arusha, Dar es Salaam, Julius Nyerere, Kilimanjaro, Olduvai Gorge, Serengeti Plains, Zanzibar.*

Index